CHURCH
AND
STATE
IN
CANADA

CHURCH
AND
STATE
IN
CANADA

ALBERT J. MENENDEZ

Prometheus Books
59 John Glenn Drive
Amherst, New York 14228-2197

Published 1996 by Prometheus Books

00 99 98 97 96   5 4 3 2 1

Library of Congress Cataloging-in-Publication Data

Menendez, Albert J.
    Church and state in Canada / Albert J. Menendez.
       p.   cm.
    Includes bibliographical references.
    ISBN 1–57392–079–7 (cloth : alk. paper)
      1. Church and state—Canada. 2. Canada—religion—20th century.
3. Canada—Politics and government—1945–   I. Title.
BR570.M46   1996
291.1'77—dc20   96–3037
                                      CIP

For Shirley

Contents

Foreword by Edd Doerr   9

Preface   11

1. Introducing Canada: A Brief History
   and a Portrait of the Provinces   13

2. Church, State, and Education   47

3. The State of the Churches   69

4. A Portrait of Canadian Religion   75

5. Abortion Rights   85

6. Sunday Closing Laws   93

7. Religious Rights of Employees   99

8. Free Exercise of Religion   101

9. Religious Establishment   105

10. Religion, Politics, and Moral Issues   109

11. Divorce and Other Matters   121

12. Canada and the United States:
    A Summary Comparison   125

Notes   129

Suggestions for Further Reading   137

Foreword

Religion, religious liberty, freedom of conscience, and relationships between religion and government are important issues in the history of every society. In one way or another these issues affect the life of every single person. Sometimes societies and governments are benign and tolerant. At other times intolerance, bigotry, persecution, violence, and conflict are promoted or allowed by governments. The conditions of religions (broadly defined to include world views or life stances not regarded by some as religions), religious liberty, freedom of conscience, and religion/government relations vary enormously from place to place and from one time to another in patterns of bewildering complexity.

Most readers of this book will be familiar to a greater or lesser degree with conditions in the United States. A majority of Americans have at least some vague notion that this country enjoys a greater degree of religious freedom than other countries under a constitutional arrangement known as "the separation of church and state," and most are at least somewhat aware of controversies, court cases, and political battles over such matters as school prayer, proposals for tax support of religious private schools, and reproductive rights.

Americans for Religious Liberty has sought to illuminate these issues in American life in a series of books listed at the end of this volume. But even persons quite familiar with religious liberty and church-state matters in the United States seldom have any knowledge of how these issues are handled in other countries. One cannot really understand and either appreciate or seek to improve one's own society without knowledgeably comparing it to others.

In this book Albert J. Menendez, research director for Americans for Religious Liberty, explores these issues in our closest neighbor, Canada.

Mr. Menendez is eminently qualified for this task. An indefatigable researcher and veritable "walking encyclopedia," he is the author of thirty books, with several more on the drawing board. He has done election analyses for ABC and NBC News and is regarded as one of the country's leading experts on religion and voting patterns in the United States.

Edd Doerr
Executive Director
Americans for Religious Liberty

☘

Preface

This monograph seeks to interpret and understand the Canadian experience of church-state relationships. It is not meant to be exhaustive or in any way the last word on the always complex and often subtle interaction between political and religious institutions.

I have looked at formal and informal relationships between religion and public life, from the constitutional framework to the general religious culture within which interaction developed.

Since this portrait is designed primarily to acquaint U.S. residents with the ways in which church and state interrelate in our friendly northern neighbor, it is inevitable that some comparisons between the two nations will be made. Americans, including the author, tend to know far too little about the Dominion of Canada, with which we share a long border and a history of relative friendship and cooperation. I hope that this overview will further understanding and will increase knowledge of the subject on both sides of the border.

I am grateful for the assistance of several individuals. My friend John Clubine of Toronto has been unfailingly helpful in providing information and insights over the years. His interest in church-state relations and his support for this project have been much appreciated. Karnik Doukmetzian, general counsel of the Seventh-day Adventist Church in Canada, has helped to clarify my understanding of the unique Canadian approach to church-state relations. So has Gerry Chipeur, an attorney specializing in human rights issues. I am indebted to them for helping me to understand the legal framework undergirding the Canadian model.

Once again, I want to express my appreciation to Marie Gore, whose skills and practical suggestions have improved the manuscript immeasurably.

Albert J. Menendez

1

Introducing Canada:
A Brief History and a
Portrait of the Provinces

Canada is the world's second largest country, comprising 3,990,456 square miles. It stretches 3,223 miles from east to west and extends southward from the North Pole to the United States border. Its seacoast includes 36,356 miles of mainland and 115,133 miles of islands.

Politically, Canada is a constitutional monarchy with a parliamentary system of democratic government. Its head of state is Queen Elizabeth II, who is represented by a Governor General. Its head of government is the prime minister. The parliament, located in the capital city of Ottawa, is bicameral.

Canada is a prosperous, literate nation with advanced systems of medical care, education, and welfare. It belongs to the United Nations, NATO, and, since 1931, the British Commonwealth of Nations. Its peacekeeping forces are found in trouble spots throughout the world. Its population in 1995 is about 29 million. The population density is seven per square mile, and 77 percent of Canadians reside in urban areas.

The nation has two official languages, English and French. About 62 percent of Canadians speak English at home, while 25 percent speak French and 13 percent converse in other languages. About 40 percent of Canadians are of British stock while 25 percent claim French ancestry. Other nationality groups have contributed to the country's cultural mosaic. A substantial number of Portuguese and Italians reside in Toronto, and many Chinese immigrants live in Vancouver. Immigrants from India and the Caribbean are numerous. About 55 percent of the population in the Kitchener-Waterloo area of Ontario are of German descent. In Newfoundland many residents trace their heritage to Ireland and to the West Country of England, and accents reminiscent of Devon and Cornwall are common. In Canada there are 330,000 native Indians and 27,000 Inuit (Eskimos), as well as 400,000 Métis, who are of mixed Indian-European heritage. These Native Canadians constitute 4 percent of the population, and are dominant in the Yukon and the Northwest Territories. They often prefer the designation "First Nation." As in the United States, most live on government reserves.

Canada is known for its passion for ice hockey, even though its official national sport is lacrosse. The Toronto Blue Jays baseball team won the World Series in 1992 and 1993. Many Canadian novelists and short-story writers have a worldwide reputation, e. g., Margaret Atwood, Morley Callaghan, Mordecai Richler, Robertson Davies, Farley Mowat, Gabrielle Roy, and Marie-Claire Blais, among others.

Canadians have given to the musical world pianists like Glenn Gould and singers like Gordon Lightfoot, Joni Mitchell, Neil Young, Buffy Sainte-Marie, k. d. lang, and Anne Murray.

Canadian actors popular in the United States include Raymond Burr, Michael J. Fox, Raymond Massey, Leslie Nielsen, Donald Sutherland, William Shatner, Christopher Plummer, and Kate Nelligan.

Now let us look at Canada's historical development. Canada's original residents were the Native Indians, who were divided into several major groups, largely as a result of their geographical location. Hunting, fishing and agricultural pursuits were dominant in this culture. Distinctive linguistic patterns and social relationships developed among these indigenous groups.

European immigration and exploration began in the sixteenth and seventeenth centuries, though there is evidence for an earlier visitation from Vikings (Norse) around 1,000 C.E. Viking explorers from Greenland and Iceland may have settled in northern Newfoundland.

In 1534 Jacques Cartier reached the gulf of the St. Lawrence River and claimed the surrounding area for France. A century later another explorer, Samuel de Champlain, settled Quebec City and Montreal. By 1663 Canada had become a province of France. About sixty thousand French had settled in eastern Canada and were making forays into what is now the U.S. Midwest. Fishing and fur-trading were the economic mainstays. Incidentally, the name Canada probably derives from a Huron-Iroquois word, *Kanata*, meaning "village" or "small community."

The British were also interested in the New World for economic reasons. The Hudson Bay Company had established outposts in present-day northern Ontario by 1670. By 1713 they controlled parts of Nova Scotia (New Scotland) and Newfoundland. Conflict between the two superpowers was inevitable. Three inconclusive wars were fought between 1689 and

1748: King William's War, Queen Anne's War, and King George's War. North America's future was settled by the Seven Years' War (the French and Indian War to many Americans) from 1756 to 1763. A turning point in this struggle was the dramatic British victory on the Plains of Abraham near Quebec City in 1759. Both the victorious British commander, General Wolfe, and his defeated French counterpart, the Marquis de Montcalm, lost their lives in this important battle. France surrendered Canada to Britain by the 1763 Treaty of Paris. The American colonies had also given support to Britain.

The young George Washington was involved in this conflict. Writes William A. DeGregorio:

> In 1752 Washington received his first military appointment as a major in the Virginia militia. On a mission for Governor Robert Dinwiddie during October 1753–January 1754, he delivered an ultimatum to the French at Fort Le Boeuf, demanding their withdrawal from territory claimed by Britain. The French refused. The French and the Ohio Company, a group of Virginians anxious to acquire western lands, were competing for control of the site of present-day Pittsburgh. The French drove the Ohio Company from the area and at the confluence of the Allegheny and Monongahela rivers constructed Fort Duquesne. Promoted to lieutenant colonel in March 1754, Washington oversaw construction of Fort Necessity in what is now Fayette County, Pennsylvania. However, he was forced to surrender that outpost to superior French and Indian forces in July 1754, a humiliating defeat that temporarily gave France control of the entire region. Later that year, Washington, disgusted with officers beneath his rank who claimed superiority because they were British regulars, resigned his commission. He returned to service, however, in 1755 as an aide-de-camp to General Edward Braddock. In the

disastrous engagement at which Braddock was mortally wounded in July 1755, Washington managed to herd what was left of the force to orderly retreat, as twice his horse was shot out from under him. The next month he was promoted to colonel and regimental commander.[1]

To pacify the French Catholic community, Parliament passed the Quebec Act in 1774. It granted a protected status to the Catholic church, assured religious liberty for Catholics, extended the use of French civil law to the courts, and extended political and voting rights to the French. Colonial America, however, saw the move as hostile to their interests and interpreted the religious provisions as the establishment of Roman Catholicism on the borders of what was then a strongly and almost uniformly Protestant area. Protests were predominant throughout the colonies, and many historians believe the passage of the Quebec Act was a major factor in the movement for American independence. The Declaration of Independence includes the Quebec Act as one reason for the break with Britain, condemning King George III: "For abolishing the free system of English laws in a neighboring province, establishing therein an arbitrary government, and enlarging its boundaries, so as to render it at once an example and fit instrument for introducing the same absolute rule into these colonies." During the American Revolution, Canada remained a bastion of Loyalists and a target for colonial American wrath.

After the American colonies won their independence from Britain in 1783, about fifty thousand American Loyalists settled in Canada, mainly in New Brunswick, Nova Scotia, and Ontario. This migration added considerably to the British-descended population.

During the next several decades, immigrants from England,

Scotland, and Wales settled in parts of Canada. In 1812 Lord Selkirk established a settlement of Scottish immigrants in the Red River Valley area of present-day Manitoba. Explorers such as Simon Fraser, David Thompson, and Sir Arthur Mackenzie paved the way for development in the West.

Another clash between the United States and Britain, the War of 1812, involved Canada. Elements in the United States wanted to take over Canada, and an invasion was mounted. Several battles were fought between the two nations until a truce was declared in 1814. For Americans this was the second war of independence, but for Canadians it was a war for survival against American domination.

By the 1840s Upper and Lower Canada, now called Ontario and Quebec, were developing societies, with governors and inchoate political institutions. Each had developed a separate culture and each sought more independence from London. The battle cry was "responsible government," in reality a search for home-rule status. This was an unsettled time and included some outright rebellions and political agitation. Responsible government was first achieved in Nova Scotia.

The British, not wanting to lose their last stronghold in North America, settled on a compromise. In 1867 the British North America Act was passed by Parliament. It established dominion status for Canada, which then included Ontario, Quebec, Nova Scotia, and New Brunswick. A central government was created in Ottawa, though significant powers were reserved to the provincial legislatures. The act served as a kind of constitution and offered admission to the then developing other regions. Canada's first prime minister, Sir John Alexander Macdonald, took office, governing a nation of 3.5 million people, most of whom were engaged in agriculture.

The remainder of the century was characterized by economic development, especially in the West, spurred on by the completion of the Canadian Pacific Railway and by immigration from abroad.

By 1912 British Columbia, Saskatchewan, Alberta, Manitoba, and Prince Edward Island had become part of the Dominion. Canada was a loyal part of the Allied coalition in both World Wars in the twentieth century. Relationships with the United States improved over time, and a considerable cross migration between the two North American giants can be seen in the census data.

One noteworthy event in Canadian and U.S. history is the Underground Railroad. This movement, which smuggled slaves out of the jurisdiction of the United States Fugitive Slave Laws, brought many African Americans to St. Catharines, Ontario.

A Maryland-born slave, Harriet Tubman, escaped into Pennsylvania as a teenager and vowed to bring as many slaves out of the U.S. South as possible. Because Upper Canada passed a law restricting slavery in 1793, the same year the United States enacted its first Fugitive Slave Act, many fugitive slaves headed north to freedom. Susan E. Merritt writes, "Canada became the only place where escaped slaves could live in freedom because escaped slaves could not be removed from Canada against their will. So after 1850, all routes of the Underground Railroad traveled north into Canada."[2]

St. Catharines became the last stop on the Underground Railroad. As a result, the town had a large black population centered around the British Methodist Episcopal Church, which remains today. (Incidentally, a group of black Loyalists settled near Halifax, Nova Scotia, after the American Revolution.)

Another African American, Mary Shadd Carey, born in the slave state of Delaware in 1823, fled to Canada and established schools in Windsor, Ontario. Thousands of American blacks, free and slave, joined them after a new and stringent Fugitive Slave Law was enacted in 1850, which allowed Southern authorities to search for escaped slaves in the free states of the North. Mary Shadd Carey was the first black woman in North America to establish and edit a weekly newspaper, the *Provincial Freeman*. As a result of these efforts, by 1860 there were two thousand African Americans living in Chatham and Buxton, Ontario.

An estimated forty thousand black Americans fled to Canada, though about two-thirds returned to the United States. As the *Washington Post*'s Charles Trueheart discovered:

> Of the forty thousand American blacks estimated to have fled to Canada, about two-thirds went home, or sent their children home, to fight for the Union Army, or later to make a new life on more familiar, and less chilly, soil. The rest, a hardy few, took root in Canada, and most of them in Nova Scotia, on the Atlantic Ocean. Of those who chose Ontario, some of their settlements are still extant after a century and a half. A few of their communities are still visibly home to people who call themselves African Canadians, though dispersion and intermarriage have taken their toll.[3]

Since World War II, Canada has been occupied with questions concerning its national identity and the preservation of its unique cultural attributes. Many Canadians are perturbed by the fact that 40 percent of the country's industry is owned by non-Canadians.

The question of Quebec remains central to Canada's future. Quebecers have always felt themselves to be victims of discrimination. In 1917 many opposed the imposition of the military draft. By the 1960s the Quebec separatist movement was gaining steam. Increased linguistic rights, cultural autonomy, and perhaps even political secession from Canada were discussed openly as options. French President Charles DeGaulle's dramatic paean, "Vive le Quebec Libre," in the late 1960s symbolized the reawakening of Quebec nationalism.

In 1976 the Parti Québécois won the provincial elections, and many Canadians anticipated the breakup of their country. But cooler heads prevailed, especially that of the nation's immensely popular prime minister, Quebecer Pierre Elliot Trúdeau. A 1980 referendum in Quebec found most residents opposed to independence. But the issue has surfaced again in the 1990s. The Bloc Québécois, the federal party supporting independence, swept the province in the October 1993 general election, and the provincial separatists won a narrow victory in 1994. Canada's present prime minister, Jean Chrétien, is a Quebecer, and the province has contributed several prime ministers to Canada's political history.

Since the defeat of the Meech Lake Accord, which some Anglo-Canadians saw as a last-ditch attempt to appease Quebec, the fear of the breakup of Canada has been accentuated.

Another internal question of some urgency involves the 330,000 Native Canadians and the 27,000 Inuit people. Concern for the survival of Canada's original inhabitants and for the transition of their posterity in the context of a highly complex society has become a major political issue. In their excellent book on contemporary Canada, Mark Lightbody and Tom Smallman observe:

Native Indian leaders have since the early 1980s become more political, making stands on constitutional matters, land claims, and mineral rights. Today a range of national organizations such as the Assembly of First Nations keep Native-

Canadian interests from being pushed aside. It is through these channels, however slow-moving, that the Native-Canadian voice will be heard in the future. Most Canadians now feel the aboriginal peoples have had a raw deal and sympathize with many of their complaints.

This, however, has not so far resulted in the introduction of many concrete attempts to improve the situation. Both provincial and federal governments are finding it less and less possible to ignore the state of affairs, and many issues regarding Native-Canadian rights and claims are currently before the courts. Among the many issues to be dealt with is some form of self-government for aboriginal peoples. Native-Canadian schools to provide control over religious and language instruction and a Native justice system are being discussed."[4]

A brief thumbnail sketch of Canada's provinces will help to place this vast nation in some geographical perspective.

Alberta

Alberta is one of the Western Prairie Provinces. Its population of about 2.5 million makes it the fourth most populous province. Entering the Confederation on September 1, 1905, Alberta was vast and sparsely populated. Today, it has two of the largest metropolitan areas of the country, Edmonton and Calgary, and prospers from its wheat farms, cattle ranches, mineral deposits, and tourism industry. Alberta has two thousand hours of sunshine per year—more than any other province—and the most varied topography.

Edmonton, the capital, is Canada's fifth-largest city and the northernmost city of its size in North America. It boasts the world's largest shopping mall in West Edmonton, a self-contained city complete with a roof, eight hundred stores, a hotel, a water park with a beach, and more. Edmonton became the oil capital of Canada in the 1970s during the oil boom days. It had been called "the gateway to the North" after the discovery of gold in the Yukon in 1897, and Edmonton became the last out-post for the gold rushers.

Edmonton's boom days subsided in the 1980s with a steep fall in oil and grain prices. About twenty-five thousand Native Indians live in the city. North America's first mosque was erected here in 1938.

Alberta's other large city, Calgary, is a meat-packing and transportation center, as well as a "cowboy metropolis," sometimes compared to Dallas or Denver. It is one of the fastest growing cities in Canada, becoming the headquarters for 450 oil companies and home to more Americans than any other place outside of the United States. A downturn in the oil and gas industries hurt the city, but the Winter Olympics of 1988 was a boon.

Alberta is fiercely conservative in politics, resembling Texas or the South. But its brand of conservatism is populist and anti-elitist. The Social Credit party originated here, and voters have since preferred either the Conservatives in good times or the Reform party in bad. Observers point to an independent, individualistic rancher mentality in the province. At times, this rightist mentality goes to extremes. Some of the more lurid anti-Semites and Holocaust-deniers have sprouted up in rural Alberta.

British Columbia

British Columbia, the westernmost province, is third in population, with about 3.2 million people. It entered the confederation on July 20, 1871. It is known for spectacular scenery from the Rocky Mountains to the Pacific Coast. Its cultural tolerance, laid-back lifestyle, and relative secularity resemble the neighboring U.S. states of Washington and Oregon. Its lifestyle has also been compared to that of California.

British Columbia is also a film center, and every day Hollywood filmmakers are somewhere in the province, usually in bustling Vancouver, the nation's third-largest city. British Columbia is prosperous, and its economy is growing at a faster rate than those of the other provinces. Forestry is British Columbia's largest industry, employing 18 percent of the workforce. Tourism is important, contributing $4.5 billion to the Canadian economy. More than five million tourists visit British Columbia annually. Mining contributes $4 billion to the economy. Canada's most unionized workforce is here (37 percent of workers belong to unions), and unemployment and recession are not unknown.

British Columbia's largest city, Vancouver, is a haven for tourists and business people. It has two universities (University of British Columbia and Simon Fraser) and extraordinary visual beauty. Culturally diverse Vancouver's Chinatown is well known.

The province's capital is Victoria, which lies at the southeastern end of Vancouver Island. Victoria has a British ambience, and the Union Jack flies as frequently as the Canadian flag. Hotels and resorts observe afternoon tea.

Politically, British Columbia is marginal, electing provincial governments from the right and left. There is a great deal of Native-Canadian culture throughout the province.

Manitoba

Manitoba, which joined the confederation in 1870, has a population of about 1.1 million. Manufacturing, food processing, and clothing factories are major sources of income, as are wheat and mineral deposits. Its original inhabitants were Cree and Assiniboine Indians. In 1812 Scottish and Irish immigrants settled the area.

Louis Riel, a controversial figure, is often considered the father of Manitoba. Riel was born in St. Boniface, which even today is the largest French-speaking community in Western Canada, in 1844. He led the Métis, a people of mixed Indian and French ancestry, in an uprising against the government in 1869. The Métis feared that their culture would be diluted when government officials opened up new land to settlers. While their revolt failed, it led to the creation of the Manitoba province. Outspoken Louis Riel was elected to the House of Commons but was forbidden to serve.

Riel's later life is shrouded in mystery. His execution of an Ontario Orangeman, Thomas Scott, made him unpopular among English Canadians. He took refuge in Montana and returned to Canada to lead another rebellion in 1885. This time he was tried and executed in Saskatchewan as a traitor. According to Lightbody and Smallman, "The act triggered French anger and resentment toward the English that has not yet been forgotten. Riel is now considered the father of the province."[5] Riel is buried at St. Boniface Basilica.

Winnipeg, the capital of Manitoba, has about 650,000 residents and, while it is in the geographical center of Canada, has a distinct Western flavor. Its gritty ambience and ways of making a living resemble those of Chicago, to which it is often compared. Like Chicago, it has many industrial workers and civil servants, whose heritage is Eastern European. A large Ukrainian population lives here, symbolized by the Byzantine domes of the Holy Trinity Ukrainian Orthodox Cathedral.

Another example of Manitoba's cultural diversity can be

observed in villages like Steinbach and Reinland, which were settled and are still largely populated by adherents of the Mennonite faith.

New Brunswick

New Brunswick, one of the original four provinces of the Canadian Dominion, has about 725,000 residents. It is Canada's only officially bilingual province (though the nation, of course, is). Nearly 37 percent of the population are of French descent. It borders Maine, with which it has much in common. New Brunswick is one of the Maritime or Atlantic provinces, and it is on Atlantic time, one hour ahead of eastern standard time.

New Brunswick was a center of Loyalist sentiment during the wars with the United States. Its capital is Fredericton, settled in 1783 by American Loyalists. It remains a placid and charmingly pro-British enclave, containing a university, an Anglican cathedral, and a tradition of such crafts as pottery, woodcarving, and pewter-smithing.

The largest town is Saint John, an industrial and port city. Canada's first incorporated city, Saint John was called "the Loyalist City" at the time of the American Revolution. During the third week of July, Loyalist Days are still observed. A few miles south of Saint John lies Campobello Island, the summer home of Franklin D. Roosevelt. America's thirty-second president spent much of his childhood there, and was stricken by polio while vacationing there in 1921. Today the Roosevelt Cottage and the Roosevelt Campobello International Park are symbols of United States-Canadian cooperation.

Also in this province is the Acadian Peninsula, briefly home to thousands of French settlers who were expelled by the British from Nova Scotia in the eighteenth century. Celebrated by the American poet Longfellow in *Evangeline,* the tragic saga of the Acadians is another link between Canada and the United States. Today's Acadian descendants largely dominate the southern part of Louisiana, preserving centuries-old cultural traditions. The Cajun country of Louisiana is often called Acadiana.

The town of Moncton, settled originally by Pennsylvania Germans, is the site of the only French university outside of Quebec.

Newfoundland and Labrador

Vast but sparsely populated Newfoundland did not become part of Canada until 1949. A rugged land influenced by the sea, Newfoundland has always lived and died by the fishing industry. In recent years the depletion of fishing stocks has increased unemployment. The Grand Banks, a series of submarine plateaus, is one of the world's great fishing grounds. Biologists, government officials, and fishers are working to find ways to replenish the declining fishing stocks.

Newfoundland is an island, and it has its own time zone, which is a half hour ahead of Atlantic time. Sales taxes are 12 percent, the highest in Canada.

Labrador is a cold and isolated region inhabited mainly by First Nation Inuit peoples. Most of the population resides along the coast of Newfoundland, which has fjords, bays, and coves.

The province has a notable aviation history. Gander was a major link for Allied planes refueling on their way to World War II Europe. The first American bombers sent to Britain left here in February 1940. Commercial airline flights have also used Gander since the 1930s.

The provincial capital, St. John's, situated on the Avalon Peninsula, is considered the oldest city in North America, and

England's first overseas colony. John Cabot arrived here in 1497. The British had to fight off the Dutch and French during the next three centuries until their rule was finally established.

Most of Newfoundland's 568,000 residents are of English or Irish descent, and religious divisions were sharp at one time. The political culture was in fact largely shaped by religious differences. Much of this separation has been reinforced by religiously segregated schooling.

The Catholic church in Newfoundland was hammered by a shocking revelation that first appeared in the St. John's *Sunday Express* on Easter Sunday, of all days, in 1989. Editor Michael Harris told the story of the sexual and physical abuse of a young man that had taken place years before at the highly respected Mount Cashel Orphanage, since 1900 a prominent institution run by the Christian Brothers, an Irish religious order that specializes in the education of young men. It was also financed by the public.

This shattering tale eventually led to a full-scale Royal Commission conducted by retired Ontario Supreme Court Justice Samuel H. S. Hughes, which uncovered collusion between the province's justice department and Catholic officialdom to cover up decades of child abuse by some of the Christian Brothers.

As in the United States, the Canadian Catholic church's response to the crisis appeared ambivalent and hesitant. Inquiries and condemnations were seen as timid and as much too late. Eventually, Newfoundland's Archbishop Alphonsus Penny was forced to resign in 1990, and Mount Cashel Orphanage was closed that year. Award-winning journalist Michael Harris writes in his book-length investigation:

> Although the Roman Catholic Church in Newfoundland had tried to distance itself from the scandal at the orphanage, stunning testimony in the dying days of the commission doc-

umented that, as early as 1954, the Archbishop of St. John's had been made aware of the sexual abuse of a boy at Mount Cashel. Although Archbishop Alphonsus Penny initially resisted calls for his resignation, he did express regret for the way in which the church had abdicated its responsibility to victims of priestly abuse and to their families.[6]

Harris adds:

> Mount Cashel Orphanage was about to become a household word across the country—a synonym for horrendous crimes of sex and violence against children and a tainted justice system that, instead of dealing with the perpetrators under the law, had secretly chosen to let them go.[7]

The Newfoundland scandal led to investigations in other provinces. The *Toronto Star* revealed that in 1960 government investigators confirmed allegations of physical and sexual abuse of residents at St. Joseph's training school in Alfred, Ontario. The two offending Christian Brothers were removed from the institution, but no charges were brought against them and not a word of the scandal was made public.[8]

Canada's 129 Catholic bishops were "completely overwhelmed by the controversy raging over sexual abuse by the clergy,"[9] observes Harris.

While criminal trials for eight Christian Brothers eventually made their way through the legal system, the underlying tragedy of church-state collusion and silence has never been directly confronted, according to Harris, an award-winning journalist. Four royal commissions in three different provinces revealed conflicts of interest between government and ecclesiastical officialdom to deny justice to the abused. Says Harris, "This is the story of a conspiracy of indifference, the human tragedy it engendered and its long overdue exposure under the disbelieving eyes of the nation."[10]

Harris says the scandals "rocked the island to its very foundations" because Newfoundland is "a fiercely sectarian society with a long history of denominational education."[11]

The revelations angered the Catholic community, which, says Harris, "struggled with the systematic failure of the church to face the reality of sexual abuse by its own clergy. This kind of reflexive self-interest on the part of church leaders fueled the anger of Newfoundland's Catholics."[12]

This scandal also broke the silence on a long history of church-state collaboration in the province. Relates Harris:

> For generations there was an unwritten rule in Newfoundland that crimes involving the clergy were best dealt with in the backrooms of the justice system—misplaced homage to the church's enormous prestige based on its innumerable good works. It was also testament to the immense political power of the pulpit in Newfoundland, a cultural reality dating from the island's earliest colonial beginnings.[13]

A four-hour fictionalized dramatization of the scandal, "The Boys of St. Vincent," was made in Canada in 1992 and aired on television in the United States in early 1995.

Nova Scotia

Nova Scotia, with a population of 900,000, was one of the four original members of the Canadian confederation. Manufacturing and shipbuilding are important to the economy, as is fishing, though the decline in fish stocks has hit Nova Scotia hard.

Canada's first permanent European settlement, founded by

Champlain in 1604, is located at Granville Ferry in Annapolis Royal. The English defeated the French here in 1710 and changed the town's name from Port Royal to Annapolis Royal in honor of Queen Anne.

The Acadians, as the French settlers called themselves, maintained their independence from both French and English governments. The region's political control changed hands repeatedly until the 1713 Treaty of Utrecht made Acadia part of English Nova Scotia. The Acadians were generally left alone for forty years until a new governor, Charles Lawrence, demanded that they take an oath of allegiance to the British Crown. When they refused, all fourteen thousand Acadians were deported. Villages were burned, and families were uprooted after centuries of living in the area. Sent first to New Brunswick, the Acadians scattered to the United States, the Caribbean, and even to the Falkland Islands, although some eventually returned to Nova Scotia and New Brunswick. According to Lightbody and Smallman:

> Today, most of the French people in Canada's Atlantic Provinces are the descendants of the expelled Acadians and they are still holding tight to their heritage. In Nova Scotia the Cheticamp area in Cape Breton and the French Shore north of Yarmouth are small strongholds. A pocket in western Prince Edward Island and the Port au Port Peninsula in Newfoundland are others. New Brunswick has a large French population stretching up the east coast past the Acadian Peninsula at Caraquet and all around the border with Quebec. There has recently been an upsurge in Acadian pride and awareness and in most of these areas you will see the Acadian flag flying and museums dealing with the past and the continuing Acadian culture.[14]

The name Nova Scotia—Latin for New Scotland—is derived from the Highland Scots who arrived on Cape Breton Island in 1773. A flourishing Scottish culture was established, and Gaelic is still spoken in some areas.

Nova Scotia's capital, Halifax, is a busy seaport and the largest city east of Montreal. It was used as a British naval base during the wars with the United States. Halifax, according to Lightbody and Smallman, "was the home of Canada's first representative government, first Protestant church, and first newspaper. Residents are known as Haligonians."[15]

The Bay of Fundy is known for the world's highest tides. Coal mining was historically the main economic activity in the town of Springhill, also the birthplace of singer Anne Murray. Unemployment is a problem in this area.

Fishing and mining are the main economic activities on Cape Breton Island, which resembles the Scottish Highlands, from which many of its residents and their ancestors migrated. Cape Breton also has an Acadian community, as well as a college offering Gaelic language courses, the Gaelic College of Celtic Arts and Crafts.

Ontario

Ontario is Canada's largest province in population. Ten million Canadians—almost 40 percent of all—reside in what is geographically the center of the nation.

The nation's capital, Ottawa, is located here amidst the trappings and panoply of Parliament, the Supreme Court, the National Gallery, and the embassies. The prime minister lives at 24 Sussex Drive, and the governor general lives around the corner at 1 Sussex Drive. Ottawa has a significant French-speaking population, bordering as it does Hull, Quebec.

The province's capital and Canada's largest city is Toronto, where 2.6 million reside. In one generation Toronto has been transformed from a drab, closed-on-Sunday kind of town, to a cosmopolitan, world-class city, which boasts as many distinct ethnic neighborhoods as New York City. Both economically and culturally, Toronto is Canada's premier city.

Ontario has a diverse economy. Manufacturing is strong. Hamilton is an iron and steel town, while Windsor and Oshawa resemble Detroit as automobile production centers. Rural Ontario has rich agricultural lands. The Niagara Peninsula is a wine-producing region. Sudbury produces a quarter of the world's nickel.

Politically, Ontario is historically conservative, owing perhaps to its large Protestant population of English and Scottish descent, although the local government at Queen's Park has occasionally been in the hands of Liberals or New Democrats. In national elections Ontario voters are very unpredictable. At the last federal election the Liberals won a landslide.

Prince Edward Island

With just 130,000 people, Prince Edward Island, which entered the Dominion in 1873, has the smallest population of the ten provinces. It is, however, densely populated.

The original inhabitants were the Micmac Indians, who still make up about 4 percent of the island's population. They are a branch of the Algonquin nation.

Prince Edward Island is primarily dependent on farming, especially of potatoes, but also has a thriving seafood industry. The island is known for its lobster suppers. The low population and geographic location contribute to a relaxed, old country kind of environment.

Prince Edward Island's most famous person is probably writer Lucy Maud Montgomery, author of the perennial favorite, *Anne of Green Gables*, a bestseller worldwide since its publication in 1908. Sightseeing tours include the areas highlighted in this popular novel which has been translated into thirty languages.

Prince Edward Island's capital is Charlottetown, established in 1763. It still retains a colonial flavor. In 1864 it was the location for discussions which ultimately resulted in the creation of the Dominion of Canada.

Tiny Prince Edward Island made history in March 1993 when voters elected the first woman premier of a provincial government, Catherine Callbeck. (Shortly thereafter, Kim Campbell became Canada's first female prime minister.)

Quebec

The province of Quebec has always been unique. In effect, it has formed a state within a state since its creation by French immigrants and explorers. Its inhabitants spoke a language different from other Canadians and adhered to a religion not shared by most Canadians.

When the French ceded Quebec to Britain in 1763, the province had only sixty thousand residents, all of whom were Catholic. Quebec adjusted harmoniously to British rule, especially after the Quebec Act was passed by Parliament in 1774. This anomalous action, adopted by a very antipapal government, bestowed a number of formal rights on the Catholic church as an institution. It was given the right to tithe its members and to own land. Catholic citizens received equal civil rights. French civil law and British criminal law coexisted. The result, says historian Mark A. Noll, "was the continuation of British rule over French Canada and the preservation of an increasingly well-entrenched Catholic culture."[16] Noll writes, "Catholicism in Quebec remained spiritually and intellectually conservative. It continued to take its orders from the pope, it aspired to a nearly medieval control over the lives of French Canadians, and it promoted a piety based on traditional rather than modern Catholic practices."[17]

The church also exercised political power in the late nineteenth century. Politically liberal Catholics, called Rouges, wanted no clerical interference in politics. Historian Kenneth McNaught describes the church-state conflict of the 1860s and 1870s:

> Taking his cue from Pope Pius IX, Bishop Bourget of Montreal led a fearsome crusade against the Rouges. Pastoral letters warned against the secularizing sins of Liberalism. . . . The bishops went forward on all fronts. Endorsing a Catholic program which condemned the doctrine of separation of church and state, they asserted and exercised the right of continuous and direct intervention in the political process. Pastoral letters and sermons thundered against the sin of liberalism, endorsed Conservative candidates, and even threatened loss of the sacraments to those who defected. The more moderate members of the clergy who doubted the wisdom of this extremism were drowned out by a chorus of ultramontane piety. The man who was to do most to reverse this unhealthy trend was a rising Liberal politician, Wilfrid Laurier."[18]

Laurier was to become Canada's John F. Kennedy. A progressive, he supported cultural tolerance and separation of church and state and became Canada's first Catholic prime minister in 1896.

Quebec Catholics were devoted to an ultramontane vision of Catholicism. They supported the most rigorous interpretation of church laws and customs. Unlike France, which moved slowly toward a Gallican type of liberal Catholic identity, Quebec remained a bastion of conservative rural Catholicism, much like Ireland and Poland. Ethnic identity was closely linked to religion, and French Catholics who resided in Ontario, Manitoba, and New Brunswick shared similar values. As Noll observed, "A climate of mutual suspicion, exacerbated by political and education-related conflict as well as by the basic differences between the two varieties of Christian faith, colored almost every aspect of Canada's religious life."[19]

The church strongly influenced both popular culture and education. As early as 1694 a bishop attempted to ban Molière's play *Le Tartuffe*, which satirized religious hypocrisy. In 1753 another bishop urged Catholics to shun secular and impious books. As historians John A. Dickinson and Brian Young observed:

> These deeply conservative bishops tried to repress sexuality and popular culture, and relegated women to a separate and subordinate sphere. The bishops opposed theatres, lotteries, mixed pilgrimages, amusement parks, carnivals, baby contests, and dancing by young people. Girls were not to attend public gatherings, and women were not to wear jewelry or watches.[20]

This was still true in the mid-twentieth century. "The power of the church hierarchy over social and intellectual life remained strong, governing Sunday activities and laws concerning theatres and cinemas."[21]

The church's influence on education was immense. The Education Act of 1875 gave every bishop in the province a seat on the public school board, which, in effect, was a Catholic school system. In this way the church sought to shape education into a means whereby religious goals were advanced. "The church was particularly able to use its control over education to recruit the best students to the clergy."[22]

The church also attracted a large number of women into religious communities. In 1921 an astounding 9.1 percent of single women above the age of twenty were nuns.[23] Dickinson and Young attribute this to church influence in education and also to a desire among some young women to avoid the rigors of married life, which by law was dominated by the husband and in which birth control was forbidden. They write, "Religious communities were an important institutional means for women to advance socially, personally, and intellectually, and offered a celibate existence as an alternative to motherhood. The convent was also an important source of material security for unmarried women."[24]

By midcentury nearly half of all elementary teachers and 85 percent of secondary teachers were nuns or brothers. The church "continued to control curriculum and textbooks and resisted an extension of compulsory education that would reduce the responsibilities of the family and increase the power of the state."[25]

The church's influence also extended to the publishing world. Quebec publishers were unable to print any books listed on the Vatican's Index of Forbidden Books, at least until the 1940s.[26] Also, "The traditional dependence of Quebec publishers and booksellers on clerical patronage for textbook purchases and large volume sales added to the church's censorship clout."[27]

This was the way of life in Quebec just before the Quiet Revolution. "The power, influence, and numerical strength of the Roman Catholic church peaked in the 1950s. With over eight thousand priests and some fifty thousand members of religious communities, the church was a daily presence in the lives of Quebecers through its control over Catholic education and health care as well as parish life."[28]

A strongly clericalist government also supported the

church's aims. It was established by a strong politician, Maurice Duplessis. The Duplessis government was so authoritarian that many liberal Catholics finally spoke out against the near church-state union in Quebec. Two priests at Laval University blasted the government in a 1956 article which concluded:

> An electoral period like that through which we have just passed becomes an instrument of demoralization and de-christianization. That which makes a country Christian is not first and foremost, the number of churches, the pious declarations of politicians, the apparent temporal or political influence of the church, or the good relations between Church and State. It is primarily the respect for truth, justice, integrity of conscience, the respect for liberty. The existing electoral proceedings are a frontal attack on all these values.[29]

Two superb novels convey the flavor of Catholic Quebec as well as any historian's accounts. They are Willa Cather's *Shadows on the Rock* (Knopf, 1931) and Louis Hemon's *Maria Chapdelaine* (Macmillan, 1921).

Quebec remained a closed society until the 1960s. Protestants and Jews found the province an uncongenial place, except in the tonier neighborhoods of Montreal and its suburbs, where many Anglicans and Jews congregated. Interfaith relations were cordial as long as certain distinct boundaries were accepted, and the Catholic majoritarian ethos was unchallenged. More militant Protestants, of the evangelical and Baptist stripes, found conflicts inevitable. (The Huguenots, who had worshiped openly and participated in early colonial life, were essentially driven from Quebec in 1627, fully fifty-eight years before their liberties were restricted in France itself.)

Cracks in the church-state wall began to occur during the

1940s. People moved to the cities to find work and joined unions to work for improved living conditions. In 1943 education was made compulsory. In 1960 Quebec's labor unions broke their connection with the Catholic church and the more secular Liberal party won a decisive election victory. In 1964 a provincial Ministry of Education was created, and the Catholic church's direct control over schooling was ended. Church control of social welfare institutions eased, then ceased.

Noll describes the province's recent history:

The most important Christian story in Canada since World War II was the revolution of Catholicism in Quebec. The revolt for more secularity and for more choices and options in personal life has been labeled "The Quiet Revolution" because it happened almost overnight but in a way that was direct and natural, with support from all sectors of society. Church attendance plummeted, as did vocations to the priesthood and religious orders. Almost overnight, it seemed, a stable synthesis of Catholic, French, rural, conservative, isolationist, and precapitalist values had disappeared. In May 1980 Quebec voters rejected a move toward secession from Canada, but the former Catholic-cultural synthesis was nonetheless gone forever. Earlier weaknesses in the Church's response to modern intellectual and social arrangements as well as the powerful inroads after World War II of market forces help to account for Quebec's rapid change.[30]

Another view is expressed by Peter Nichols, a London *Times* correspondent who has specialized in Vatican politics and Roman Catholic affairs. He wrote in 1981:

The Church was banished from its place in institutionalized society and, at times, must have looked near to extinction. For instance, the 1971 national census showed that twelve times as many inhabitants of Quebec said they did not believe in God, compared with the 1961 census. . . . But the French-Canadians turned on their own church when the revolution came, casting it aside as one of their oppressors and so the Church lost its hold over society.[31]

Interestingly, most church leaders in Quebec accepted the changes. Few seem to dream of a restoration of clerical power. Adds Nichols:

During the period of disengagement when the Church turned over welfare work and schools to the state, there were never violent attacks on the Church nor resistance from the Church to disengagement. We are now facing the first generation of highly educated French-Canadians. Despite the drop in attendance at Mass, the bishops did not panic. Women are becoming active in French-Canadian parish life. Two are chancellors of diocesan courts.[32]

The decline of clerical control in Quebec has coincided with an improvement in the legal status of women. In 1940 women were granted the right to vote in provincial elections. (Women could vote all over Canada in federal elections beginning in 1917.) The first woman elected to the legislative assembly was Claire Kirkland-Casgrain, in 1961. In 1964 women were recognized as equals to men in Quebec's civil law, and married women received the right to administer and dispose of their own property. Divorce was legalized in 1968. In 1975 the Quebec Charter of Human Rights and Freedoms recognized the equality of spouses in marriage. Two years later the old concept of "paternal authority" in marriage was abolished, and, the following year, the civil code was amended to mandate the equal distribution of family property when a marriage is ended by divorce or separation.[33]

At the same time holy days such as All Saints' Day and the Immaculate Conception were dropped as public holidays. From 1966 to 1988 the number of nuns declined from 34,571 to 22,525 and the number of priests diminished from 8,758, to 6,428.[34]

A contemporary novelist has explored the challenges facing the church in modern Quebec. Marie-Claire Blais's *Mad Shadows* (McClelland & Stewart, 1971) and *A Season in the Life of Emmanuel* (Farrar, Straus & Giroux, 1980) are extraordinary evocations of the modern spirit in conflict with tradition.

One example of the decline of a Catholic ethos in Quebec is the refusal of juries to convict Dr. Henry Morgentaler, a courageous physician who challenged the province's antiabortion laws. On repeated occasions he was arrested by authorities for the "crime" of performing an abortion, and each time juries refused to send him to prison. Abortion is now legal, accepted, and relatively widespread in Quebec. Family planning is popular. Quebec, which once had the highest birth rate in Canada, now has the lowest.

The language controversy and the separatist movement, which wants Quebec to be a nation separate from Canada, overshadow church-state issues, even in education, though at times the issues intersect. In 1968 the Catholic school board of the Montreal suburb of St. Leonard tried to deny English language instruction to the largely Italian population, but riots ensued, and the provincial government introduced a bill allowing parents to choose the language in which their children were to be educated. Later, in 1982, a Nationalist government tried to deny English language instruction in Quebec Protestant schools, resulting in a suit against the government by the Quebec Association of Protestant School Boards. Quebec's Superior Court ruled in the school board's favor.

The rise of separatism and the possibility of Quebec's secession from Canada have reduced its appeal to immigrants. While Quebec contains 25 percent of the country's population, only about 15 percent of Canada's immigrants choose to live there.[35]

The immigration controversy briefly developed a religious twist in November 1990 when Michael Pallascio, chairman of the Montreal Catholic School Commission, issued a statement urging the government to recruit those immigrants "who share with us the Judeo-Christian values." It appeared to be an appeal for a religious test for immigration, and the province's minister of immigration, Monique Gagnon-Tremblay, denounced the suggestion as "totally unacceptable" because it would violate the religious freedom guarantees of the Canadian Charter of Rights.[36] The secular and religiously neutral nature of Quebec society was reaffirmed.

Quebec still has many English Protestants who reside in the townships and in Westmount, an affluent suburb where French Canadians, Jews, and Scottish Presbyterian bankers live in relative amity, according to the province's most celebrated writer, Mordecai Richler. Jews are strong in the D'Arcy and McGee riding, and many Hasidic Jews reside in Outremont. The Jewish community, however, has declined from 120,000 to 95,000 in Montreal since 1970.[37]

Joseph Fletcher of the University of Toronto and the Institute for Social Research of York University carried out a survey in 1987 which found that anti-Semitism was more prevalent in Quebec than elsewhere in Canada. The prejudice was alarming. Said Fletcher in a 1989 address to the Canadian Jewish Congress, "While anti-Semitic sentiments are present in every region of the country, they are disproportionately concentrated in the province of Quebec. In this rather ominous sense, Quebec is truly a distinctive society."[38]

A 1984 National Election Study confirmed these findings of a Francophone tendency toward dislike of Jews. While 10 percent of English Catholics and 14 percent of English Protestants expressed anti-Semitic attitudes, 24 percent of French Catholics did so.[39] A survey conducted over a seven-year period by Taylor Buchner, a professor of sociology at Concordia University in Montreal, discovered that a quarter of Quebec residents harbored anti-Jewish attitudes, and that 20–25 percent of Quebecers said they would not vote for a Jewish candidate of their own political party. Fully 26 percent of Quebecers said Jews had too much power in Canada, compared to 19 percent of all Canadians who felt that way.[40]

Richler also cites an early nationalist newspaper, *Le Devoir*, which "advocated the deportation of Jews already settled in Quebec or, failing that, at least denying them Canadian nationality, revoking their right to vote, furnishing them with special passports, and establishing ghettos."[41]

Quebec continues to attract immigrants from French-speaking countries like Haiti and Lebanon, but 35 percent of recent immigrants eventually left the province for other regions of Canada. Since 1945, two-thirds of the three million immigrants to Quebec had left.[42]

Saskatchewan

Saskatchewan, which lies just north of Montana, has a population just under a million, and entered the confederation in 1905. It is farm country, the greatest grower of wheat in North America. Culturally and politically, it resembles Minnesota—liberal on economic matters, moderately conservative on social and cultural issues.

Saskatchewan was the center of Canada's socialist move-ment. The Cooperative Commonwealth Federation (CCF) was founded in the province's capital, Regina, in 1933 by farmers, la-borers, and intellectuals. It was an outgrowth of the Progressive movement, which was strong throughout western Canada and the United States from the turn of the century to the Depression. By 1944 the CCF formed the government of Saskatchewan under T. C. Douglas. It emphasized social reform and legislation that improved the lives of working people. The CCF govern-ment was popular with voters and remained in power for twenty years. Its policies were very much like those of the Min-nesota Democratic Farm Labor party. In 1961 the CCF became the New Democratic party, which occasionally wins provincial elections, but has never formed a national government.

Ironically, left-of-center Saskatchewan contributed one of Canada's most conservative prime ministers, John Diefenbaker, a courtroom lawyer from Prince Albert, who became prime minister in 1957 and was reelected in a historic 1958 landslide. Even Quebec supported this likeable populist Tory.

Saskatchewan has a rugged, individualistic character. It is the only province that does not recognize daylight savings time in summer.

The Yukon and Northwest Territories

With a population of 31,500, the Yukon Territory lives up to its image as a desolate outpost bordered on the north by the Beau-fort Sea in the Arctic Ocean. The Yukon is almost entirely cov-ered by mountains. The original inhabitants are Athapaskani and Inuit, though they make up only one-seventh of the pre-sent population.

The Yukon was initially part of the Northwest Territories,

but became a separate territory in 1898. Two years before, gold was discovered in a tributary of the Klondike River. The gold rush transformed the area, and thirty-eight thousand gold diggers hurried to Dawson City, the first capital, to find their fortunes. The gold soon ran out, and more mundane industries such as mining, fishing, and forestry were established. In 1953 the capital was transferred to Whitehorse, where a majority of Yukon residents now live. Today, tourism ranks second to mining. The Yukon's main road is the Alaska Highway, built in 1942 by Americans and Canadians. Both poet Robert Service and novelist Jack London lived for a time in the Yukon and celebrated some of its unique inhabitants.

The Northwest Territories, with its capital at Yellowknife, has a population of 57,700, most of them Inuit or Dene Native Canadians. Many adventurers, seeking the Northwest Passage and the North Pole, have ventured into these frozen parts over the centuries.

The discovery of oil and radium in the 1920s and 1930s brought changes to the region, as did the building of airfields and weather stations. Gold was discovered near Yellowknife in 1934.

Canada and the United States still have not resolved questions relating to sovereignty of the far north regions. But one area of contention was resolved on November 12, 1992, when the Inuit signed an agreement with federal and provincial authorities called the Nunavut Accord. This treaty will result in a new territory, to be called Nunavut, by 1999. One-fifth of Canada's land surface will become a new political designation. It will also be officially bilingual, with Inuktitut and English as the recognized languages.

2

Church, State, and Education

Education in Canada is very much a local prerogative. It is controlled by the ten provinces rather than by the federal government. Consequently, patterns of educational financing, legal rights of Protestant and Catholic and private schools, and the status of religious activities in the nonsectarian tax-supported schools are all matters of local prerogative. One study concluded:

> In Canada, education comes under provincial jurisdiction at least partly because the designers of the Canadian Federation believed that education was a problem area best kept out of the national arena. Differences in culture, religion, and language required decentralized responses if consensus was to be achieved. The end result is that Canada possesses an array of public and private educational institutions and arrange-

ments that vary along regional, class, religious, racial, ethnic, and linguistic lines.[1]

Let us begin with Ontario.

Ontario

Ontario, called Upper Canada at its beginning in the early eighteenth century, had only denominational schools. In the 1840s government officials considered the establishment of public tax-supported education. At that time the Anglican bishop of Toronto, John Strachan, requested that the legislature grant public funds for the support of denominational schools. This became the pattern for all religious groups in Ontario. By the 1860s though, most non–Roman Catholic churches had lost interest in maintaining separate schools, and began to consider public education favorably. The Separate Schools Act of 1863 placed the Catholic schools on an equal basis with the "common" schools in terms of funding.

According to the terms of the British North America Act of 1867, Canada became a confederation with a government separate from the United Kingdom. In order to reach a compromise settlement between French-speaking Quebec and English-speaking Ontario the founders of the Canadian confederation adopted Article 93, which provided that Roman Catholic separate schools in Ontario, where Catholics were a minority, would always receive public funding. (The same compromise guaranteed that Protestants in Quebec, where they were in a minority, would also have equal funding for their educational institutions.) Section 93 stated: "Nothing in any such law shall prejudicially affect any right or privilege with respect to denominational schools which any class of persons have by law in the province at the union."[2]

Consequently, Ontario's Roman Catholic schools received a kind of privileged status from the beginning. They were not totally funded but they received more and more funding. Originally, the Catholic schools were funded through the eighth grade, then to the tenth grade, and finally, by 1984, full funding all the way through the last year of senior high school became the norm.

Article 93 of the 1867 law was maintained in the Constitution Act of 1982, under which Canada operates today. The same act also has a Charter of Rights and Freedoms modeled to some extent on the United States Bill of Rights. However, Ontario's unique and generous aid to Catholic schools was held to be an integral part of the Canadian constitution after challenges were mounted.

In 1984 Ontario Bill 30, which provided for the full funding of Catholic schools, was passed over strong objections from Protestants, Jews, Humanists, and nonreligious citizens who believed they were discriminated against since only Catholic schools and public schools are supported by tax funds in Ontario. Private Protestant and Jewish schools receive no funding and opponents of Bill 30 charged unequal treatment of the law and discrimination against those who wanted to establish private schools outside the Catholic sector. The bill was sponsored by the Progressive Conservative government in Ontario, which had been the traditional party of the Protestant majority in the province, and many voters angrily saw this as a kind of sell-out for political reasons. Several human rights and civil liberties groups, including the Canadian Civil Liberties Association, the Ontario Secondary School Teachers Association, the Coalition for Public Education, and the Hindu Federation challenged the constitutionality of Bill 30. However, the Ontario Court of Appeal in 1986, by a vote of 3 to 2, held the bill constitutional. The Supreme Court of Canada concurred the following year. However, several justices on both courts concluded that the funding of Catholic schools, and the failure to fund Protestant or Jewish schools, did violate the Canadian Charter of Rights, particularly Section 2A, which guarantees freedom of conscience and religion, and Section 15, which guarantees equality to all Canadian citizens. A great deal of interfaith disharmony emerged at this time, and the late Anglican Archbishop Garnsworthy of Toronto was particularly outspoken in his criticism of the complete funding of Catholic schools.

Only one member of the provincial legislature, Norman Sterling, a Progressive Conservative from Carleton-Grenville, spoke against Bill 30 in 1986. In an impassioned address, Sterling said, "I do not believe the state should voluntarily pay to indoctrinate children in one religious belief to the exclusion of all the others. Ontario is a pluralistic society and is becoming more so every day. Our society will not tolerate bigotry, racism, or discrimination. Bill 30 clearly discriminates in favor of one religious group over all other religious groups."[3]

Here is how the Ontario system works. Ontario has thirteen years of schooling, rather than twelve as in the United States and the rest of Canada, and the majority of Catholics attend what is called the separate school system. Almost all teachers in the Catholic schools are Catholic and religious requirements are normative. Very few non-Catholics (only about 2 percent) attend the Ontario Catholic schools. The vast majority of Catholic School students are English-speaking, a small number are French-speaking, and an even smaller number are Ukrainian.

Since the nonsectarian public schools are not permitted to discriminate against teachers on the basis of religion, only Catholic teachers have access to all schools. They are given favorable treatment in Catholic school hiring practices, and are also eligible to teach in the public schools. But there are almost no teachers in Catholic schools who are not Catholic.

In Ontario, there are about 552,000 students in the Catholic separate school system, and these schools have grown 66 percent since 1978. There are 479,000 pupils in English Catholic schools and 73,000 in French-language separate Catholic schools in the eastern and northern parts of Ontario. In effect there is a kind of church-state collusion to force Catholic parents to send their children to Catholic schools.

Each separate school board has from seven to twenty-eight trustees, elected for three-year terms at the regular municipal elections. Every Catholic Canadian citizen of age eighteen or above, who by choice is enumerated as a separate elector, may vote and stand for election in his own municipality. In other words, local secular elections also include races for the Catholic school board.

Under Ontario law every Catholic head of household may assign the municipal property tax of the house or apartment which he owns or rents either to the public school system or to the separate Catholic school system. That source provides about one-quarter of the funds that school boards require. The rest comes through a complex formula from the provincial government. As the Rev. Carl C. J. Matthews, former chairman of the Toronto Separate School Board, wrote in 1990, "For Ontario Catholic schools in 1988, the total revenue per elementary pupil averaged $4,383 and for secondary $5,589. None of that came from the Church."[4]

The Catholic schools in Ontario have a kind of "have-your-cake-and-eat-it-too" mentality. They lobbied for years to complete the full funding for senior high schools. The government of Toronto even arranged for public high school buildings to be transferred to the separate school system, which created anger and bitterness and very poor interfaith relations throughout the province. It even led to demonstrations in some cities and occupation of public schools that were scheduled for transfer to separate schools. The relationships between Protestants and Catholics deteriorated sharply in those towns where public schools were transferred to the Catholic school boards. From 1985 to 1991 forty-three public schools throughout Ontario were transferred to the Catholic Separate School Boards.

In the town of Amherstburg, violence erupted when public school protesters confronted police and occupied the grounds of the General Amherst public school in 1991. The school, which had eight hundred students, was scheduled to be turned over to the Catholic school system, which had four hundred students. For a few months public and parochial school students shared the school and it was called General Amherst and St. Thomas of Villanova. The Essex County Board of Education, under pressure from the provincial government, tried to force the school to be turned over to the Catholic school board. Violence and anger broke out throughout the town and a Catholic church was firebombed. A tentative agreement called for the public school board to build a new Catholic school—at public expense, of course—but the situation is still problematical.[5]

Catholic school interests are still not satisfied despite having some of the most generous funding of any country in the world. Father Matthews complained, "Parity of funding is the goal, but a separate school pupil, on average, across the province, is still supported by 10 percent less than [a] public school neighbor."[6]

Another problem comes in the question of the faculty in Catholic schools. The 1986 bill which provided for complete funding of Catholic schools required that in 1995 Catholic school boards must hire any qualified non-Catholic who applies for employment, provided the applicant promises to respect the philosophy of the Catholic school. Catholic authorities objected to this compromise. Matthews wrote, "Our parents believe that the Catholic faith cannot be handed on by a teacher who does not live that faith. The Canadian courts have always upheld the Catholic character of Roman Catholic separate schools, so parents and educators are confident that the infamous Section 136 1.a will be repealed before it comes into effect."[7]

Matthews continued, "Since faith is better caught than taught, the teacher who is eager to share that faith becomes the vital link in living and learning."[8] The Catholic schools receive every type of benefit imaginable. There are courses given to improve the religious education training for Catholic schools, and those courses for advance credit are recognized by the Ministry of Education.

Despite the near collusion of state and church to force Catholic parents to send their children to Catholic schools, some resolutely refuse to do so. While 38 percent of Ontario is Catholic, only 28 percent of all students are enrolled in the separate schools. This means that somewhat over one-fourth of Catholic parents refuse to send their children to separate schools, preferring the public schools. As might be expected, only 3 percent of students in Catholic schools in Ontario are non-Catholic, and virtually no teachers are.

Five Jewish parents filed suit in 1991 challenging the government's refusal to extend equal funding to their schools. They charged that this was discriminatory and unconstitutional. Supported by the Canadian Jewish Congress, they filed suit in December 1991 in the Ontario Court of Justice. On August 4, 1992, Justice William Anderson rejected the claims and the remedies sought. He admitted that the parents' rights to religious freedom and equality under the Charter of Rights were being violated, but felt that it was not up to the courts to redress the grievances. He suggested that the legislators should reconsider the funding question. This produced a great deal of criticism throughout Canada among people who wondered why courts were not regarded as the appropriate bodies to interpret the constitutionality of laws passed by legislators. Many Canadians have charged that the Ontario system violates not only the national constitution, but also international standards of human rights, to which Canada is a signatory.[9]

In July of 1994 the Ontario Court of Appeal ruled that denial of funding for Jewish and Protestant schools does not violate the Canadian Charter of Rights and Freedoms. However, on February 2, 1995, the Supreme Court of Canada announced that it would hear arguments on extending public funding to more than two hundred non-Catholic religious private schools in Ontario. This development was hailed as "a major step forward" by the Ontario Multi-Faith Coalition for Equity in Education, a coalition representing Hindu, Muslim, Sikh, and fundamentalist Christian parents who want religion taught in public schools.[10] Supporting the seventy thousand students now attending non-Catholic private schools would cost between $156 million and $340 million per year.[11] Government lawyers argue that financing the schools would lower educational quality and "fragment society along religious lines,"[12] as if the present arrangement did not already do that.

The attitude of Roman Catholic authorities has not been helpful, and raises questions about the commitment of Roman Catholic leaders to ecumenism and positive interfaith relations. The Rev. Carl Matthews, in attempting to explain the Ontario school system to American Catholic teachers, who held their national convention in Toronto in April 1990, crowed that, "Did I mention that the taxpayer foots the bill and that almost all teachers are Catholic? In April, when American Catholic teachers come to the Archdiocese of Toronto they will see something amazing—schools that are at the same time devoutly Catholic and entirely funded by the taxpayer."[13] Matthews dismissed the protests of Protestants and Catholics who objected to the transferral of public schools to the Catholic school system. He commended the government for "arranging some fine, public high school buildings to be transferred to the separate Catholic school system. The screams of protests for that action have now vanished and peace seems to have come to the province."[14]

The Catholic school system's close connection to the state has caused some problems for the church's leadership. On August 29, 1994, the Metropolitan Toronto Separate School Board reinstated Joanna Manning, a teacher who had been barred from teaching religion in Catholic schools in September 1992 because of her criticism of church teachings on birth control and the ordination of women. She had been forced to give up the headship of a religious education department because of her views (which are shared by substantial numbers of practicing Catholics in Canada and elsewhere). At the arbitration hearing, Manning was supported by the Ontario English Catholic Teachers Association.[15]

Manning, a founder of the Coalition of Concerned Canadian Catholics, which favors women's ordination, optional celibacy for clergy, and the popular election of bishops, still faces opposition from the hierarchy. Toronto Archbishop Aloysius Ambrozic has intimated that her reinstatement would be a threat to the future of Catholic education in the province. The *Toronto Star*'s education reporter, Rita Daly, got to the crux of the issue in her report: "School board officials acknowledge their concerns go deeper. They say Manning's win poses a serious threat to the Catholic system's constitutional rights and the future of publicly funded separate schools in the province."[16] Manning was reinstated by the entire school board.[17]

Attempts to inculcate conservative values in Catholic school children seem to have fallen short of the goal, according to sociologist Reginald Bibby. His comprehensive survey of twenty-five hundred Canadian teenagers found that Catholic school students held similar—and predominantly liberal—views on sex-related matters. Bibby concluded, "Our examination of students in the Roman Catholic systems suggests that, even when religious groups attempt to increase their influence by operating their own schools, they are experiencing very modest amounts of success."[18]

A small Protestant private school system, which is run generally by the Christian Reformed Church, has continued to challenge the discriminatory funding. The private Protestant schools, whose students make up about 3 percent of the 1.9 million students throughout the province, have challenged the system of funding only Catholic schools. The Ontario Alliance of Christian Schools, representing seventy-three private schools, made its case before the Ontario Court of Appeals in September 1993. Justice David Doherty expressed reservations about the impact of financing independent schools because he did not want the educational system to be splintered into "cultural ghettos. "However, that is essentially what Ontario schools are like now.[19]

Many Ontario residents continue to oppose vigorously the present school situation in their province. The Friends of Public Education in Ontario, a group based in Harrow, issued a report by Renton H. Patterson in 1992 which concluded, "The Constitution does not bind the province to fund separate schools. . . . It is not only possible, but increasingly imperative, for the Ontario government to abolish public funding of separate schools."[20]

Some spirited and angry Ontario residents vented their feelings in the 1990 provincial elections when 75,462 of them (8 percent of the voters in thirty-two ridings—equivalent to U.S. congressional districts) voted for a hastily-organized minor party called Confederation of Regions (COR). The COR was the only party to challenge the separate school aid.[21] They also tended to represent Anglophone voters opposed to multiculturalism.

Ontario's public schools, incidentally, no longer may require religious exercises, instruction, or formal prayers in classrooms, as a result of a 1990 Ontario Court of Appeals ruling.

All of Ontario's schools, public or private, must teach essentially the same curriculum, which assures a degree of consistency and uniformity.

Quebec

Quebec is Canada's second largest province in population, and is almost entirely French-speaking, as well as 88 percent Catholic. It has no public school system whatsoever. It has a Catholic school system and a Protestant school system. The Catholic system has about 90 percent of the total student enrollment and is mostly French with only a few English schools in the English-speaking parts of Montreal. The remaining 10 percent of the students attend the Protestant school system, which is mostly English. About 20 percent of the Protestant students are in French-language schools. Jews living in the province and those who have no religious affiliation usually choose one of the sectarian school systems, and generally prefer the Protestant schools. Non-Christians, however, cannot become trustees of the Protestant schools.[22] Glenn noted that five thousand Jewish students attend private (nonfunded) Jewish schools in Quebec.[23]

The government of Quebec has tried for a decade to realign education along linguistic lines. Quebec requires all immigrants to attend French-language schools (public) unless they came from English-speaking countries. But private schools can accept students from all backgrounds. Bill 107, which passed in 1988, was declared constitutional by the Quebec Court of Appeal. Bill 102, a revised version of the first bill, was passed by the National Assembly of Quebec (provincial legislature) in 1990. It was immediately appealed to the Supreme Court of Canada by five denominational school boards in Quebec. The Supreme Court upheld that decision on June 17, 1993, in *Quebec Association of Protestant School Boards et al.* v. *Attorney General of Quebec* (1993) SCJ 68. The Rev. Carl J. Matthews charged that passage of this bill "would mean the death of Catholic schools for English-speaking families in the Montreal area and, arguably, the mortal illness of Catholicity in French schools across that province."[24] Considering the decision of the court in the Ontario school funding controversy, it would appear unlikely that Quebec could make these changes. However, the status of Quebec as a part of the Canadian confederation itself is uncertain.

Quebec maintains 213 Catholic and 31 Protestant school districts. Says Glenn, "Generally members of all non-Catholic groups—Jews, Muslims, Hindus, and the nonreligious—enroll their children in the Protestant schools."[25]

Quebec's "Catholic" public schools are "run by committees to which both the Ministry of Education and the Catholic bishops appoint representatives,"[26] he adds.

Under Quebec's Private Education Act of 1968, three types of private schools are available, most of them Catholic-oriented. Those deemed "of public interest" receive per pupil grants of 85 percent of the rate given to public schools and may not charge tuition amounting to more than 50 percent of the grant. The "recognized for grant purposes" schools receive per pupil grants of 60 percent of the public school rate. A third category of "schools under permit" receive no government aid but are subject to oversight by the Ministry of Education.[27]

The language question now supersedes religion as a matter of controversy. Most immigrants prefer English-language instruction, and in 1973 about half of the enrollment in Montreal's English Catholic schools were children of Italian ancestry. But the historic pattern remains firm because 92 percent of students in Protestant schools are taught in English, while 94 percent of those in Catholic schools are taught in French.[28]

Multiculturalism is raising issues in Quebec. About fort thousand Muslim students attend Montreal schools, and prin cipals in some Catholic schools have expelled girls who wea distinctive Islamic dress, particularly the *hijab* for females. Human rights groups have protested these incidents.[29]

The Quebec Teachers' Federation has called for religious integration of Quebec schools and for the dropping of the required religion classes. The 126,000-member QTF represents the Catholic school faculties. In Protestant schools most references to religion are included in history classes.[30]

British Columbia

British Columbia is the least Catholic province; only about 19 percent of its population are members of the Catholic church. British Columbia resembles Washington and Oregon in its large nonreligious population. About 30 percent of British Columbia residents stated that they had no religion in the last census. The schools are mostly public, though there are Catholic schools and private Protestant schools. About 50 percent of the operational costs of private schools in British Columbia for many years were provided by the provincial legislature. That increased to 80 percent in 1991. The public schools are nonsectarian.

Public subsidy of church schools in Canada is now complete. The last holdout, substantially secular, prosperous British

Columbia, capitulated in 1980 when provincial officials began to pay 15 percent of all educational costs for those attending private and parochial schools. Then the subsidy rose to 30 percent. Today the government pays 50 percent of all expenditures of church-run schools. Since it costs provincial taxpayers about $3,500 a year per pupil in public schools, the subsidy now totals $1,750 per pupil in private and parochial schools. The annual total is about $350 million. Tuition fees and parish subsidies make up the remainder, according to Annette Yonge, spokesperson for the Vancouver Catholic School Board.

Whether that 50 percent figure will eventually be raised is uncertain. Yonge indicated that the province's late archbishop opposed any additional support, but the previous tendency of governments throughout Canada to expand the nonpublic school subsidy suggests otherwise.

Canadian education, like its U.S. counterpart, is largely a local or provincial concern. (Canada's provinces are similar to U.S. states.) Each province jealously guards its educational policies, and Canada's constitution does not specifically prohibit tax aid to sectarian institutions. In any event, Canada's 1982 Charter of Rights and Freedoms would not supersede arrangements arrived at prior to or as a result of confederation, as for example in Quebec, where there are only state-funded Catholic and Protestant schools. There are no public schools in Quebec or Newfoundland. Ontario has a curious system, whereby Roman Catholic separate schools are now guaranteed full funding comparable to public schools but Protestant or other religious schools are denied funding. It is all part of Canada's checkered history of conflict and accommodation between English Protestants and French Catholics. These antiquated relationships, however, are less meaningful in a nation that is increasingly pluralistic, with growing numbers of Buddhist, Muslim, and Hindu citizens, as well as Jews and Eastern Orthodox Christians. In addition, 11 percent of Canadians call themselves agnostics or atheists. And nearly half of Canadian Catholics are not of French descent; many are English, Italian, Portuguese, or of other national backgrounds.

British Columbia is the least Catholic and the most secular province. Roughly 30 percent of its residents declared "no religion" at the last census, and about 7 percent listed "other" religions than Christianity. About 20 percent are members of the United Church, a 1925 union of Methodists, Congregationalists, and most Presbyterians. Just under 20 percent are Roman Catholic, and 13 percent are Anglican. The Anglican church has suffered the most serious declines, since it was the province's largest religious group from 1891 to 1951. Conservative Protestants claim about 9 percent of British Columbians, while Lutherans and those Presbyterians who refused to join the United Church claim 8 percent.

And yet even here the church school lobby emerged triumphant. The reasons seem familiar: aggressive lobbies, disillusionment by some parents with the performance of the public schools, and political capitulation. The province's strong socialist party, the New Democratic party, often wins here in federal elections, but the quirky right-wing Social Credit party was in power on the local level most of the time from 1975 to 1991. The New Democrats are against parochiaid in theory, but they no longer see it as top priority. They have battled for abortion rights, for quality medical care, and for support for Native-Canadian and women's issues. Thus, the more conservative parties were able to break the ice by establishing the principle of public support for church-affiliated schools.

Church schools are growing in popularity, perhaps as a result of the funding. Catholic schools have waiting lists, with preference for parish members and Catholic students from outside the parish boundaries. Non-Catholic students are few. Daily religious instruction is mandatory.

On the elementary school level, "the Faith is integrated into the curriculum," said Ms. Yonge. On the secondary school level religion courses are academically oriented, and credits are given for them.

If a highly educated, sophisticated, prosperous, and religiously tolerant and pluralistic place like British Columbia can accede to the blandishments of the parochiaiders, there would seem to be very few places left with the willpower or political gumption to resist.

The Independent Schools Support Act of 1977 provides public funding to private schools that "do not promote or foster racial or ethnic superiority or religious intolerance and persecution."[31] Some schools receive a government grant of 9 percent of per-pupil operating cost of the local public school district, while others may receive a 30 percent grant. Says Glenn, "The most rapid growth in this province has been that of evangelical Protestant schools," which more than tripled in number between 1959 and 1985.[32]

Alberta

Alberta is a very conservative, western, English-oriented, and predominantly Protestant province. Its public schools are non-sectarian, but it also has Catholic separate schools and some Protestant schools which are funded by the public. Alberta resembles Ontario and Saskatchewan except that Alberta does fund Protestant separate schools. It also pays up to 75 percent of the costs to the private sector schools. About 17 percent of students attend the Catholic separate schools.

Before Alberta joined the Canadian confederation in 1905,

its schools were mostly operated by churches. Under the North West Act of 1875, the new public schools were divided into Protestant and Catholic sections. The Alberta Act of 1905 guaranteed equal funding to public, private Catholic, and private Protestant schools.

School taxes are paid on a denominational basis. For example, once a Catholic separate school district has been established in a local area, all Catholic residents are taxed for that school, while those of other faith groups are taxed for the support of the public schools. This discourages Catholics from choosing public instruction. In a 1976 case, the Alberta high court ruled that it was legal to charge tuition for a child enrolled in a school other than that which was provided for his religion. Both Protestant and Catholic separate school boards are under the control of the provincial education department, as are the public schools. In 1968 independent private schools began to receive government support, often in the form of "educational services."

At present, private schools receive government grants equal to 75 percent of those provided to the public and separate schools. In 1985 about twelve thousand students attended 190 private schools in Alberta.[33] Even a Talmud Torah School, open only to those who are "committed to the Hebrew language and Jewish religious studies," became an official state-sponsored "alternative" school in Edmonton in 1975. Until 1983 Calgary's public school system included a native (Indian) school, a Hebrew school, and two Logos Evangelical Christian academies. After the 1983 local elections, the religious systems were removed from the public domain.

Alberta has had controversies similar to those involving the Amish in such states as Pennsylvania and Wisconsin. Local Mennonites and Hutterites looked askance at the increasing secularization of the public schools and removed their children to hastily built and staffed academies. They were prosecuted by local authorities in the 1970s. In Canada's equivalent to the U.S. Supreme Court decision in the *Yoder* case, Alberta's high court ruled in 1978 in *Regina* v. *Weibe* that the religious freedom guarantees in the Alberta Bill of Rights superseded school attendance laws, and that the public school instruction was incompatible with the religious faith and practices of these individuals.[34] The religious dissenters were victorious. Alberta law allows all schools to include up to fifteen minutes of religious devotion each school day, but very few, if any, do so.

Saskatchewan

Saskatchewan has a school system very similar to Ontario. It has public schools and it has publicly funded Roman Catholic separate schools. Funding from the public covers 59 percent of the costs of "approved" private high schools in Saskatchewan. However, no aid is given to Protestant schools, or to nonapproved alternative schools.

Saskatchewan funded Catholic separate elementary schools from 1905, when the province joined Canada, but did not provide funding for denominational high schools until 1964. Since then, Catholic separate schools receive equal funding with public ones. Catholic schools are under the administration of local school boards and the supervision of provincial education authorities.

A 1965 court ruling made it almost impossible for individuals to choose public schools if they belonged to a religious minority which had established its own separate school district. (So much for choice!) In effect, Catholic children, the court held, had no right to attend the common public school if a

Catholic separate school already existed in their district. As Glenn comments, "This unusual ruling illustrates the fact that the rights of religious or ethnic communities to provide education can be quite distinct from the right of individual parents to choose a school."[35]

Manitoba

Manitoba has a large nonsectarian public school system and both Catholic and Protestant private schools, though they are relatively small. About 20 percent of the funding of the private schools comes from the public sector. Manitoba had a system of separate religious schools from 1867 until 1890, when the Manitoba legislature abolished its system of denominational schools. Manitoba also allows religious instruction in the nonsectarian public schools during the last half hour of each day, a kind of released time on school property.

Since 1979 some private schools have received a degree of government funding in exchange for a measure of government supervision. Local public schools provide home economics and industrial arts programs to private schools under an informal kind of shared-time basis.[36]

Manitoba has also moved to accommodate the language requirements of its many Ukrainian- and German-speaking residents.

Newfoundland

Newfoundland, the last province to enter Canada's confederation, in 1949, has an unusual school system which resembles Quebec's. It has no public schools. Eight religious denominations have a legal right to own their own schools. The Roman

Catholic schools are the most common. In the metropolitan area of St. John's, for example, 62 percent of the students attend Catholic schools. Five other religious groups, the Anglicans, Salvation Army, Presbyterians, Moravians, and the United Church (which includes Methodists, Congregationalists, and some Presbyterians), united to establish integrated public schools with a religious basis. In St. John's about 37 percent of the students attend these schools. Two small denominations, the Pentecostals and the Seventh-day Adventists, maintain their own private schools and about 1 percent of the student population attends the Adventist and Pentecostal schools.[37]

The Pentecostals appealed to the government in 1987 to become a legal entity in the education business. In effect this was Canada's first constitutional amendment. Canada's Constitution Act of 1982 allows provinces to make changes affecting only their own governmental or educational structures to be approved by the federal House of Commons without debate from the other provinces. On June 23, 1987, the Canadian Parliament approved the rights of the Pentecostal Assemblies to run their own schools in Newfoundland. There were no committee hearings or any debates on the question. A number of human rights organizations and liberal groups questioned the process.[38] The Newfoundland-Labrador Human Rights Association has been lobbying for an end to the denominational school systems.

Kathleen Ruff, publisher of the *Canadian Human Rights Advocate*, charged that this process "means that even in 1987 government can bring in constitutional changes that violate the Charter."[39]

Glenn argues that the five churches which pooled their resources in 1969 have created "general public integrated schools which have become largely secularized."[40] He adds,

"Private schools (as distinguished from these denominational public schools) do not receive government funding, but they are subject to approval and inspection by the provincial minister of education."[41]

For administrative reasons the Newfoundland government has proposed cutting the twenty-seven school boards organized along religious lines into ten organized by geography. The plan, announced in August 1994, would save the province $10 million a year. Roman Catholic and Pentecostal officials expressed opposition.[42]

Newfoundland voters decided to end public funding of denominational schools by a 54-to-46-percent majority in a September 5, 1995, referendum. For the first time in three centuries, students will attend public schools closest to their homes rather than schools divided by religion. Despite efforts by church school officials to circumvent the will of the electorate, there is every reason to believe that the provincial government will move to implement the decision to improve educational quality, save at least $31 million per year, and reduce ecclesiastical control of education. It was significant that St. John's, the largest city in the province and 60 percent Catholic, voted 56 percent in favor of the proposed change.

Nova Scotia, New Brunswick, and Prince Edward Island

Nova Scotia, New Brunswick, and Prince Edward Island all have nonsectarian public schools with no religion-based public schools and no funding of private schools. In Nova Scotia and Prince Edward Island, authorized textbooks and curriculum materials may be provided to approved private schools, but there is no public funding. These three Maritime Provinces probably resemble the United States more than the rest of Canada in terms of education.

For several decades all three provinces had Catholic schools by "gentlemen's agreement" with local public school boards. These were public schools which functioned, in effect, as Catholic schools. But during the past three decades they have mostly disappeared.[43] Many students, however, still attend private Catholic schools, especially in Saint John, the largest metropolitan area in New Brunswick, where 58 percent of the students attend Catholic schools and 41 percent attend public schools. New Brunswick's population is one-third French Catholic.

Bergen concluded, "Most Catholic needs have been met within the public school districts due to the more or less homogeneous francophone settlement patterns."[44] New Brunswick maintained mostly denominational schools until 1871, when a public education system was established. "Local compromises and the distribution of population gave schools in some areas a French Catholic flavor," writes Glenn.[45]

This may have prevented the development of separate Catholic schools. Since 1967 consolidation and secularization have reduced the religious orientation.

Yukon and the Northwest Territories

The Yukon and the Northwest Territories have mostly public schools, but separate denominational schools are provided where requested. There are two nonfunded private schools in Whitehorse and Yellowknife.

3

The State of the Churches

Canada has always had a higher Catholic population percentage than the United States. Even in 1921 Canada was 39 percent Catholic compared to 16 percent in the United States. Since 1961 the percentages in both nations have evened out at around 46 percent in Canada and 25 percent in the United States. Protestantism has declined more in Canada than in the United States, and Catholics moved ahead of Protestants in Canada in the 1981 census and further ahead in 1991. Despite a decline of one-third, Anglicans are stronger in Canada than Episcopalians in the United States. The United States has far more Baptists and evangelicals than Canada. Both countries have vigorous Jewish and Eastern Orthodox communities. Canada also has far fewer denominations, which is partly related to Canada's smaller population (one-tenth of the U.S.).

Since 1871 Canada has included a religious question in its

decennial census, so its figures have a bit more authority or exactitude than various estimates of religious identification in the United States (see table 1). However, as Mark Noll observes, "Canadian census figures are not good indices of active membership, but they do provide a sense of religious loyalties that linger even after active participation ceases."[1]

Within Canada Catholicism is still the nominal faith of 88 percent of Quebec's population. It is also strong (more than 30 percent) in Ontario, Newfoundland, and the Maritime Provinces (New Brunswick, Nova Scotia, Prince Edward Island). And about one-fourth of the residents in the Prairie Provinces (Alberta, Saskatchewan, Manitoba) are also Catholic, many of Ukrainian ancestry. British Columbia is the least Catholic province, with only one-fifth of its population identified as Catholic. British Columbia resembles Washington, Oregon, and California, with a large percentage of its population (20 percent) adhering to no religious faith.

The United Church is Canada's middle-of-the-road Protestant denomination, founded on June 10, 1925, by the merger of Methodists, Congregationalists, and about 70 percent of the Presbyterians in the country (the moderate to liberal ones). It is relatively strong everywhere except Quebec and Newfoundland, though nationally it has declined from 20 percent in 1961 to less than 15 percent today.

The Anglican church, the Canadian branch of the Church of England and sister of the U.S. Episcopal church, has declined from 15 percent of the Canadian population in 1941 to under 10 percent today. It is still influential in cities and has a large following in Quebec and Newfoundland.

Presbyterians have lost more than half of their share of the population since 1941, but they maintain pockets of strength in Ontario and Prince Edward Island. Baptists have also declined—

unlike in the United States, where they are booming—but maintain a presence in New Brunswick and Nova Scotia. Pentecostals and the Salvation Army are strong in Newfoundland, and Lutherans are numerous in the western provinces. Ukrainian Catholics and Mennonites are prominent in Manitoba.

Church attendance—as opposed to preference—has declined considerably. Writes Noll, "The rates of church attendance in Canada, which were considerably higher than those in the States for probably the entire century before 1960, have subsequently fallen considerably below those in the States."[2] Noll explains the trends:

> In Canada, regular attendance has fallen off considerably, by Protestants from a high of 60 percent in 1946 to well under 30 percent in the late 1980s, and by Catholics from above 80 percent in the early 1960s to barely 40 percent in the late 1980s. The Catholic drop-off has been most spectacular in Quebec, where religious practice was once most secure. In 1955, the year of the first Gallup survey of Canadian religion, 93 percent of Quebec Catholics reported being in church the previous week. By the late 1980s, the proportion had fallen to nearly 30 percent.[3]

In terms of actual membership in a local congregation, the percentage of Canadians claiming membership fell from 58 percent in 1975 to 29 percent in 1990.[4]

In belief patterns, Canadians remain a religious people. Majorities say they believe in God, pray regularly, read the Bible occasionally, and believe in some kind of life after death. Still, percentages indicating affirmative religious statements have declined. Canadians are similar to Americans in what they say about religion, and are somewhat less skeptical than Europeans. Women exceed men on the religious belief and practice scale, as they do in all other countries.

Finally, polling shows sharp regional differences in Canadian religious belief and practice. Noll writes, "In Canada, church attendance and traditional beliefs are both highest for Protestants and Catholics in the Atlantic provinces and lowest in British Columbia. In this regard, the Atlantic provinces are, in effect, Canada's 'religious South,' for in the American South levels of belief and practice are also higher, on average, than in any other region of the country."[5]

In summary, then, Canadian religion has been transformed by modernity, secularization, and technological changes. Observes Noll, "Canada, a society more cohesive and deferential to authority, has experienced rapid losses in church adherence as its political, economic, cultural, and educational leaders turned from traditional faith."[6]

These changes are far-reaching and probably irreversible, he suggests. "Since World War II, the changes that have most significantly shaped North American culture have stressed technology instead of morality, personal enrichment instead of altruistic service, and the potential for individual development instead of the force of historical traditions."[7]

By way of a conclusion, Professor Noll again deserves the last word:

In French-speaking Canada, the Catholic Church's intrinsic authority is only a shadow of what it once was. In the rest of Canada and in the United States, the Protestant mainstream that once dictated cultural values, provided standards for private and public morality, assumed primary responsibility for education, and powerfully shaped the media—that Protestantism is fragmented and culturally feeble.[8]

Table 1

Canada's Religions
Figures from National Censuses*

	1941	1961	1971	1981	1991
Roman Catholic	43.4%	45.8%	46.2%	46.5%	45.7%
United Church	19.2	20.1	17.5	15.6	11.5
Anglican	15.2	13.2	11.0	10.1	8.1
Presbyterian	7.2	4.5	4.0	3.4	2.4
Baptist	4.2	3.3	3.1	2.9	2.5
Lutheran	3.5	3.6	3.3	2.9	2.4
Eastern Orthodox and Greek Catholic	n.a.	2.4	2.5	n. a.	1.4
Mennonite	1.0	.8	n.a.	.8	.8
Pentecostal	.5	.8	1.0	1.4	1.6
Salvation Army	.3	.5	.6	.5	.4
Jewish and other	n.a.	4.6	6.5	8.5	10.9
None	n.a.	.4	4.3	7.4	12.3
Population in Millions	11.5	18.2	21.6	24.3	27. 0

*Mark A. Noll, *A History of Christianity in the United States and Canada* (Grand Rapids, Mich.: Eerdmans, 1992), p. 471.

4

A Portrait of Canadian Religion

Canada has considerable diversity in religion. According to statistics from the *1992 Yearbook of American and Canadian Churches* (see table 2), Roman Catholics in Canada number about 11,375,000 and are by far the largest single religious group. In second place is the United Church, claiming 2,050,000 members. It is a member of the World Methodist Council and the World Alliance of Reformed Churches and has many more identifiers than actual members. In third place are the Anglicans with about 850,000 members. They, too, have far more identifiers than actual members. The Anglican Church of Canada is a self-governing member of the Anglican Communion. It is governed democratically by a General Synod and its leaders include a primate, Archbishop Peers; four metropolitan archbishops; and thirty diocesan bishops. These are the big three of Canadian Christianity.

Many other religious groups also claim considerable follow-

Table 2

Membership
in Major Canadian Religious Groups—1992*

Roman Catholic	11,375,914
United Church	2,049,923
Anglican	848,256
Jewish	296,425
Lutheran	286,264
Presbyterian	245,883
Greek Orthodox	230,000
Pentecostal	226,691
Baptist	130,000
Mormons	126,000
Ukrainian Orthodox	120,000
Jehovah's Witnesses	101,713
Christian Reformed	88,892
Salvation Army	88,899
Christian & Missionary Alliance	74,286
Mennonites	65,755
Seventh-day Adventist	40,047
Coptic	40,000
Orthodox Doukhobors	21,300

Yearbook of American and Canadian Churches 1992, pp. 266–69.

ings. There are 296,000 Jews in Canada, divided roughly equally among Toronto, Montreal, and the rest of the country. The first synagogue was built in Montreal in 1768. Called Shearith Israel, it was a branch of the Spanish-Portuguese congregation of London. The Canadian Jewish Congress was established in 1919 and has become an important factor in Jewish life. It helped to resettle forty thousand Jewish immigrants from Europe after World War II. Canada's record of accepting Jewish immigrants during World War II was a poor one, as the nation refused to accept most Jewish immigrants who were trying to flee from Hitler. There are 112 Jewish places of worship in Canada: 53 Orthodox, 43 Conservative, 14 Reform, and 2 Reconstructionist.

There are 286,000 Lutherans in several branches of the Lutheran community in Canada. They are most numerous in the western part of the country, as they are in the western part of the United States. There are 245,000 Presbyterians who refused to participate in the United Church and preferred their own denominational grouping. These are the more conservative Presbyterians. There are also 226,000 Pentecostals in Canada. They are particularly strong in Newfoundland, where their 31,719 members represent 6 percent of the population. The Greek Orthodox church also claims 230,000 followers in Canada. Other churches which have significant followings include the Baptists, with 130,000 members and a famous seminary, McMaster Divinity School. There are 126,000 Mormons, 120,000 members of the Ukrainian Orthodox Church, and 101,000 Jehovah's Witnesses. The landscape of western Canada is made much more scenic with numbers of onion-domed Ukrainian Orthodox and Eastern Rite Catholic churches. There are about ninety thousand members of the Salvation Army and about ninety thousand members of the Christian Reformed church in Canada. The Mennonites, who are strong in Ontario and the western provinces, claim about sixty-five thousand members in several branches. There are forty thousand Seventh-day Adventists and forty thousand members of the Coptic Orthodox Church, whose members have emigrated mostly from Egypt. There are also five thousand Unitarian Universalists in forty-two congregations and a Humanist Association of Canada.

An unusual Canadian-flavored group is the Orthodox

Doukhobors, who claim 21,300 members. This group, which originated in seventeenth-century Russia, experienced a great deal of persecution under the Russian Orthodox-Czarist regime. In 1899 about 7,500 of these so-called spirit wrestlers fled to Canada. They are pacifists, somewhat anticlerical and anti-institutional, and have an intense religious life. They follow a "Book of Life" which consists of songs and chants memorized by each generation. They have a democratically elected executive committee and their official name is the Union of Spiritual Communities of Christ. They have also split off into other groups. There is a reformed type of Doukhobors and there is an extremist offshoot called the "Sons of Freedom," who are accused of parading in the nude and burning and bombing government facilities.

The Canadian Conference of Catholic Bishops is headquartered in Ottawa and represents the political and social posture of the nation's largest religious community. There are sixty-five Latin Rite bishops and archbishops and eight Eastern Rite bishops, called eparchs. The Roman Catholic church is quite ethnically mixed, and has always been noted for its ability to include many different nationalities in its community. The same is also true for the Pentecostals, who have two hundred ethnic churches and 109 Native American churches.

There are also Muslims, Buddhists, Sikhs, and many other religious groups in Canada. The Bahai community was incorporated by act of parliament in 1949 and has about fifteen centers of worship around the country. The Buddhist Churches of Canada, a branch of Mahayana Buddhism, were founded in Vancouver in 1904. There is a growing Muslim community in the country, and the Sikhs also have many followers. The first Sikh conference was held in 1979. There are Sikh temples, called Gurdwaras, in Toronto, Vancouver, and Victoria. There are eleven Eastern Orthodox communions in Canada.

There are several Protestant denominations indigenous to Canada. The Missionary Church of Canada, which comes from an Anabaptist heritage, is a completely autonomous Canadian religious community. The Christian and Missionary Alliance was founded in Toronto in 1887 and soon spread to the United States and other parts of the world. Its Canadian branch became autonomous in 1980 and has about seventy-five thousand members. There is a small Evangelical church in Canada, headquartered in Medicine Hat, Alberta, which gained autonomy in 1970, after its U.S. branch joined the Methodists. The Pentecostal Assemblies of Canada have always tended to be more mainstream and less marginalized than their American compatriots. The Pentecostal Assemblies were incorporated under the Dominion Charter in 1919 and are recognized as an ecclesiastical corporation in Quebec.

There are eighty-nine theological seminaries and Bible schools in the country. Roman Catholics, Anglicans, and Baptists all have ten each; the Mennonites have eight; Pentecostals, six; and the United Church, five. There are five ecumenical interdenominational liberal seminaries and thirteen evangelical nondenominational seminaries There are also seminaries which belong to many other conservative Protestant communities. Despite the decline of institutional religion in Canada in terms of church attendance and identification, the number of seminarians is growing. In those seminaries affiliated with the Association of Theological Schools, the number of seminarians increased from 3,696 in 1986 to 4,647 in 1991, a gain of 26 percent. In 1993 the number reached 5,333. Canada's two largest seminaries are Regent College in Vancouver and Ontario Theological School in North York.

Many religious colleges in Canada are associated with secular universities. There are Roman Catholic faculties of theology at the Universities of Montreal, Sherbrooke, St. Michael's College at the University of Toronto, and the University of Laval, Que-

Table 3

Where Canada's Religious Groups Live
1991 Census

Religious Body	Reported Membership	Ontario	Quebec	Percent Living in Western Canada	Mari-times
Roman Catholic	12,335,255	28.7	47.4	15.9	8.0
All Protestant	9,780,710	45.3	4.1	38.6	12.0
Jewish	318,070	55.2	30.7	13.2	0.9
Eastern Orthodox	387,395	48.6	23.0	27.5	0.9
Eastern Non-Christian	747,455	50.7	13.0	35.2	1.1
No Affiliation	3,386,365	36.2	7.6	52.7	3.5
Anglican	2,188,115	48.4	4.4	31.5	15.7
Baptist	663,360	39.8	4.1	28.0	28.1
Lutheran	636,210	35.8	1.6	60.5	2.1
Mennonite	229,460	22.7	0.7	76.3	0.3
Pentecostal	436,435	38.3	6.7	37.8	17.2
Presbyterian	636,295	66.3	2.7	22.5	8.5
United	3,093,120	45.6	2.0	41.1	11.3
ALL	26,994,045	37.0	25.2	29.3	8.5

bec. There is an Evangelical church college, Regent College, associated with the University of British Columbia. There is an interdenominational Faculty of Theology at the University of Winnipeg, and the Central Pentecostal College is affiliated with the University of Saskatchewan. This has tended to integrate religious studies more into the secular curriculum, and also frees the churches from having to finance many of their own institutions.

In Alberta and British Columbia church colleges are funded from the public treasury at a rate about 70 percent of that provided to public universities. As in the United States, some church colleges have elected to go the secular route. Waterloo Lutheran University in Ontario, for example, renamed itself the Sir Wilfrid Laurier University.

There are 172 Christian and Jewish religious periodicals published in Canada. Of them, twenty are Roman Catholic, thirteen Jewish, nine Anglican, six Eastern Orthodox, and 124 Protestant. There is even an Italian Pentecostal magazine called *Voce Evangelica* published in the nation.

The 1991 census reveals the contours of the Canadian religious landscape. It also reveals the gap between reported religious identification and actual church membership, especially among Protestants. Fewer than half of Baptists, Lutherans, Presbyterians, Anglicans, and Mennonites are actually members of local congregations, when one compares church membership data to census preferences. But 93 percent of Jews and 92 percent of Catholics apparently are identified as such by local group statisticians.

There is a distinct geographical pattern to religious affiliation. Groups which are more concentrated in Ontario include Presbyterians, two-thirds of whose Canadian identifiers reside there, Jews, Eastern Orthodox Christians, Anglicans, and the various non-Christian Eastern religions such as Buddhists, Muslims, and Sikhs. Roman Catholics and Mennonites are somewhat underrepresented in Ontario, even though some rural towns like Kitchener have a Mennonite flavor.

Catholics are almost twice as likely to live in Quebec as are all Canadians, and Jews are also slightly more likely to live in *la belle province*. Protestant groups are far less likely to do so.

In western Canada live three-fourths of the nation's Mennonites and three-fifths of the Lutherans. Slightly more than half of those with no religious affiliation also reside in the West, as do 41 percent of the United Church members. Jews and Catholics are less likely to live west of Ontario. The Maritimes have large numbers of Baptists, Pentecostals, and Anglicans. Baptists are more than three times as likely to have settled in the Maritimes than elsewhere in Canada. Pentecostals and Anglicans are twice as likely to reside there. For example, while only 8.1 percent of all Canadians call themselves Anglican, fully 26.2 percent of Newfoundlanders do so. While only 2.5 percent of all Canadians are Baptists, 11 percent of the residents of Nova Scotia and New Brunswick adhere to that tradition.

The nonreligious seem to flock to British Columbia, where 30 percent of the residents declared themselves without a religious affiliation. This is more than double the figure for all Canadians (12.3 percent).

As in the United States, Canada's provinces reflect very different religious cultures and traditions.

Sociologist Reginald W. Bibby writes persuasively that Canadian religious life is undergoing major changes at a rapid pace. In his 1987 book *Fragmented Gods*, Bibby synthesized twenty years of research about Canadian religious practice. He suggested that Canadian religion is highly specialized and oriented toward consumer tastes, much like any other product, intellectual or commercial.

Bibby writes, "Religion has ceased to be life-forming at the level of the average Canadian. For most, it is extremely specialized in content and influence. . . . For the majority of Canadians, religious commitment is a former acquaintance rather than a current companion."[1]

This affects all regions of the diverse nation, he says. "Religion no longer occupies center stage in our society. Protestantism is not a pivotal feature of Anglo culture; Roman Catholicism is no longer at the heart of Québécois culture."[2]

Church attendance is the primary indicator of at least nominal religious commitment. In 1946 two of three Canadians attended church on an average Sunday. Only one in three did so in 1986.[3] Roman Catholic attendance in Quebec plummeted from 88 percent in 1965 to 38 percent in 1985. Weekly church attendance by Catholics outside of Quebec declined from 69 percent to 49 percent during the same two decades.[4]

Even when the churches were appearing to do relatively well, as in the 1950s, they were merely holding their own. Writes Bibby, "The statistical truth of the matter is that most of Canada's religious groups were essentially standing still when they thought they were enjoying tremendous growth."[5]

There has also been a decline in the percentage of Canadians who regularly watch religious radio and television.[6] These changes have also affected patterns of belief and commitment to the intellectual foundations of religion.

The impact of religion on culture is slipping. Concludes Bibby, "Religion has little influence when it comes to political and economic decision making, higher education, entertainment, and even personal morality."[7]

He continues, "When it comes to sexuality, the country's religious groups are frequently both ignored and stripped of any unique claim to authority by the committed and uncommitted alike."[8] Even Canadian evangelicals and fundamentalists have been relatively unsuccessful in the new climate. "Conservatives are no more successful than the mainline Protestant denominations in reaching people not active in other religious groups. . . . Only about 10 percent of the new members had come from outside the evangelical community, almost without exception as a result of social ties, notably friendship and marriage."[9]

Still, not all of the news is gloomy for institutional religion. Bibby says, "In the midst of the mass exodus, the paradox is that religion lives on, even showing occasional signs of health."[10] The majority of Canadians still identify with one religious community or another. The vast majority (77 percent) pray and believe in a personal God (66 percent).[11] A majority are baptized (71 percent), 52 percent are confirmed in their faith traditions, 66 percent have a religious wedding, and 46 percent a religious funeral. About a fourth send their children to Sunday school (46 percent in the Atlantic Provinces).[12]

Some additional confirmation of the changing nature of Canada's religious life comes from the Decima Quarterly Report conducted for *MacLean's* magazine. "Between 1971 and 1981, the number of atheists and agnostics in Canada climbed 70 percent. In the same decade, Buddhists showed the largest percentage increase of any organized religion: 223 percent. Pentecostals were up 54 percent; Mormons, 36 percent. On the other hand, Unitarians declined in number by 31 percent, and Doukhobors by 27 percent.[13]

Overall church attendance was 55 percent in 1965, 41 percent in 1975, and 32 percent in 1985.[14] Respect for organized religion declined in the Decima polls. In March 1980 public confidence in organized religion outweighed skepticism by 6 percent. By 1990 skeptics outnumbered those who had confidence in religion by 9 percent. "The lapse," say pollster Allan Gregg and journalist Michael Posner, "was most pronounced among men, those with only elementary education, residents of Ontario and the Atlantic Provinces, and the middle-aged."[15] These citizens may have been influenced by the reports of sexual abuse scandals among a number of Canadian clergy, especially those at the Mount Cashel Orphanage in Newfoundland.

Gregg and Posner also found that "The erosion of religious faith in the 1980s reflected a population that had lost its grip on the old verities and was searching in disparate ways for new ones."[16] Political, media, judicial, and business figures and institutions also lost community confidence during the 1980s, the pollsters discovered.

5

Abortion Rights

From its foundation, Canada followed England's common law regulation of abortion. The earliest statutory prohibition, enacted in 1869, was called "An Act Respecting Offenses Against the Person." Based on Lord Ellenborough's Act of 1803, this statute made procuring an abortion of a "quick fetus" a capital offense and provided lesser penalties for abortion before quickening. These provisions were retained in the Canadian Criminal Law Codes of 1892, 1906, 1927, and 1954. Section 251(1) of the 1954 Code treated abortion as a serious crime for which the maximum sentence was life imprisonment.[1]

In 1969 the federal Parliament, influenced by worldwide trends toward liberalization and decriminalization of the procedure, made major reforms in Canada's abortion law. In brief, the new law held that it was not a criminal offense to procure an abortion if the continuation of the pregnancy was likely to endanger the life or health of the female person. There were two requirements: (1) a majority of at least three qualified medical practitioners of an accredited or approved hospital had to certify in writing that the pregnancy would endanger the woman's health, and (2) the abortion had to be performed in an accredited or approved hospital by a physician who was certified and who did not serve on the committee which approved the abortion request.[2]

The 1969 law was seen as an improvement by abortion rights advocates but as inadequate to the needs of a changing society. One physician in particular, Dr. Henry Morgentaler, a Polish-born Holocaust survivor who practiced medicine in Montreal, defied the law by continuing to perform abortions outside an accredited hospital and without obtaining the required certificate from a therapeutic abortion committee.

Morgentaler's clinic was raided by Montreal police in June 1970, and he was charged with the crime of performing an illegal abortion. In November 1973 a jury acquitted him. But a curious law allowing courts to overrule an acquittal came into play in April 1974 when the Quebec Court of Appeal set aside the ruling and ordered him sentenced to prison. This action was upheld by the Supreme Court of Canada in March 1975, and the physician was remanded to the Bordeaux Jail for eighteen months. Three months later, he was brought before a second jury on additional charges but was again acquitted. He remained incarcerated for ten months, being released in January 1976 on bail, pending a third trial. The outrage surrounding his treatment led the federal government to introduce an amendment to the Criminal Code preventing appeals courts from reversing jury verdicts. (This was quickly christened the Morgentaler Amendment.)

A third trial was held in Montreal in September 1976, and

once again Dr. Morgentaler was set free. However, the physician had suffered a heart attack in prison and was deeply in debt. To the rescue came a surprising player: the newly elected separatist government of the Parti Québécois, led by René Lévesque, which swept into office in November 1976. Premier Lévesque's government encouraged the establishment of abortion services in hospitals, with limited success. However, the government promised not to enforce the federal criminal abortion statute. In fact, access to abortion services in Quebec became the best in Canada. The Quebec-operated community health centers started in 1980 to provide abortion services, even though this was still technically illegal.

By the early 1980s the access issue became paramount. Canada's vocal antiabortion lobby concentrated on persuading hospitals to abandon the procedure. In 1983 Morgentaler opened clinics in Toronto and Winnipeg. This decision, writes Stan Persky, "is perhaps best understood as a feature of the altered political circumstances shaped by the women's movement."[3] Once again Morgentaler and his colleagues were arrested for operating independent clinics. This case came before a Toronto jury in November 1984, and for the fourth time a jury declined to convict the outspoken and courageous physician.

The government appealed, and the Ontario Court of Appeals unanimously overturned the acquittal and ordered a new trial in October 1985. This court held that the guarantees of life, liberty, and the security of person, enunciated in Canada's 1982 Charter of Rights and Freedoms, did not apply to abortion rights. It was this judgment that was appealed by Morgentaler and his fellow physicians to the Supreme Court of Canada in October 1986, thus setting the stage for Canada's version of the landmark *Roe* v. *Wade* decision in the United States.

Canada's Supreme Court is the supreme authority in interpreting whether the Constitution and its Charter of Rights and Freedoms applied to abortion. Like the United States, Canada's Supreme Court has nine justices, but only seven heard the arguments in the fall of 1986. At issue was whether the Criminal Code's Section 251 conflicted with Section 7 of the Charter of Rights. Collateral issues were unequal access to the procedure, and the defense of necessity in cases where delay could damage the health of the woman.

The momentous decision in what was now being called the Morgentaler case was announced on a frigid January 28, 1988, at the Supreme Court in Ottawa (almost fifteen years to the day after the U.S. Supreme Court's abortion rights ruling). By a five to two vote, the Supreme Court declared that Canada's abortion law violated Section 7 of the Charter of Rights. Stan Persky says the decision was far-reaching: "In its boldest Charter case decision to date, the Court indicated unequivocally that it was prepared to use the Charter of Rights and Freedoms. Chief Justice Dickson's language was both tough and forthright." The Chief Justice affirmed,

> State interference with bodily integrity and serious state-imposed psychological stress, at least in the criminal law context, constitutes a breach of security of the person. Section 251 clearly interferes with a woman's physical integrity. Forcing a woman, by threat of criminal sanction, to carry a fetus to term unless she meets certain criteria unrelated to her own priorities and aspirations, is a profound interference with a woman's body and thus an infringement of security of the person.[4]

The majority also clarified a clause in Section 7 which implicitly justified some deprivations of life, liberty, and security of the person in those cases held to be "in accordance with the principles of fundamental justice." Abortion was not held to be one of these circumstances. Criminalizing abortion was seen as unjustifiable. Finally, the Court held that criminalizing abortion was not a "reasonable limit that could be justified in a free and democratic society."[5] All possible nuances had been considered and rejected. The decision to seek an abortion was firmly held to be a fundamental, unabridgeable, and constitutionally protected right.

The provinces immediately moved toward implementing the decision. Ontario's Health Ministry abolished the hospital abortion committees and announced that abortions would be covered under medical insurance. (The provinces administer Canada's universal medical care program.) Quebec already paid for abortions. Manitoba made abortion services more accessible.

But there were holdouts. Prince Edward Island provided no abortion services. It still does not. Some were reluctant to allow clinics to operate. British Columbia, under the very conservative regime of Bill Vander Zalm's Social Credit party, refused to provide public financing and declared that abortions would not be considered medically required unless a woman's life was endangered. Even abortions for pregnancies resulting from rape and incest were disallowed. The British Columbia Civil Liberties Association immediately appealed these decisions to the British Columbia Supreme Court. On March 7, 1988, the Province's Supreme Court struck down the government's attempt to restrict abortion availability. Declared Chief Justice Allan McEachern, "Such a determination, that abortion services are not medically required, purports to remove services that are in fact medically required from the definition of insured service. Such a regulation is invalid, being one that is not authorized by the statute and is inconsistent with the statute and with common sense."[6]

The British Columbia conflict points up the anomaly of Canada's federal system, with its heavy emphasis on provincial prerogatives. Canada has no federal abortion law. The implementation of even fundamental rights varies widely.

Dr. Morgentaler opened clinics in Quebec, Ontario, Manitoba, Nova Scotia, Newfoundland, and Alberta. When his Toronto clinic was firebombed on May 18, 1992, the Ontario government rebuilt it.

Today, 22 percent of all abortions in Canada are performed in Morgentaler's clinics. The doctor opened his eighth and last clinic in Ottawa, in sight of the Parliament buildings and Supreme Court, on October 13, 1994. He declared that the battle for abortion rights had been won. A few of the provinces still refuse to allow the establishment of clinics or refuse to pay doctors who serve clinic patients. The government of New Brunswick, for example, has gone to court to prevent clinics, asserting that only hospitals should be allowed to perform the procedure. Writes journalist Anne Swardson, "Morgentaler responds that women from New Brunswick have to travel to Toronto, Montreal, or Maine to have abortions because the local hospitals will not do them; his clinic in the New Brunswick capital, Fredericton, is operating while the case is being considered."[7]

The total number of abortions performed in Canada rose 5.7 percent between 1991 and 1992, to a total of 100,497. There are 25 abortions per 100 live births, compared to 37. 9 in the United States.[8]

While the basic legal issue seems to be resolved, the question of availability remains contentious. As human rights activist Shelagh Day wrote in 1988:

Given governments' behavior since the Morgentaler decision, the struggle for access to abortion, far from being over, may simply be in another stage. Women may need to go to court again, this time against provincial governments who fail to provide, and pay for, safe accessible abortion services for women. Cases challenging, for example, the complete lack of abortion services for women in Prince Edward Island and ongoing access problems in British Columbia and other provinces, may be in the courts in the coming months.[9]

This remains true today.

Table 4

Abortion Rates by Province—1991

Province	Abortions Per 100,000 Population
Yukon	564.5
Northwest Territories	503.2
British Columbia	333.1
Ontario	315. 0
Alberta	252.4
Manitoba	244.1
Quebec	216.3
Nova Scotia	203.4
Saskatchewan	126.3
New Brunswick	82.0
Newfoundland	75.7
Prince Edward Island	0
NATION	261.0

Source: *Statistics Canada*

About 70,463 therapeutic abortions were performed in hospitals in Canada in 1991, according to *Statistics Canada*, which also added that "figures were underreported for British Columbia."[10] The Canadian abortion rate of 261.0 per 100,000 population has actually declined since 1981, when it was 268.0. (In 1971 it was 143.3.)

The rate is highest in the sparsely populated Yukon and Northwest Territories, followed by British Columbia and Ontario. Near average rates occur in Alberta and Manitoba, while Quebec's rate is still a bit lower than the nation. Quebec, however, has experienced a significant increase in abortion rate since 1981. Nova Scotia is also below average. Low rates are recorded in Saskatchewan, New Brunswick, and Newfoundland. No abortions have been reported in Prince Edward Island since 1982, when there were six. This is a surprising development, since seventy-one abortions were recorded in 1975 in Prince Edward Island.

The social conservatism of the Maritime Provinces is noticeable. All of the Maritimes rank below the national average in divorce and abortion rates per population. Religion may indeed play a role in developing and fostering social conservatism.

6

Sunday Closing Laws

Sunday closing laws have long been a feature of the Canadian legal landscape. Following the traditions of British common law, which restricted commerce on Sunday as early as 1448, early Canadians followed suit. Upper Canada enacted An Act to Prevent the Profanation of the Lord's Day in 1845, which substantially preserved the 1677 Sunday Observance Act of the British Parliament. In 1906 Canada's federal Parliament passed the Lord's Day Act, which went into effect on the first day of March 1907. This quaint act prohibited, among other things, such activities as shooting in such a manner as to disturb public worship and the selling of foreign newspapers on Sunday. A number of provinces also enacted legislation preventing commercial activity, various forms of entertainment, and most types of nonessential work on Sundays. The Judicial Committee of the Privy Council upheld challenges to these laws in

1925.[1] The Canadian Supreme Court also upheld the law in a 1959 case.[2]

Other decisions through the years upheld restrictions on the Sunday sale of alcoholic beverages,[3] railway travel,[4] and theatrical presentations.[5]

In 1963 a case involving individuals convicted on a charge of operating a bowling alley on Sunday reached the Supreme Court. The appellants contended that the Canadian Bill of Rights, R.S.C. 1970 App. III, should render the Lord's Day Act inoperative. The Court majority rejected this view, holding that violations of Sunday closing laws constituted a part of criminal law and could only be changed by parliamentary decision. Even in this decision the majority acknowledged that "complete liberty of religious thought" and "the untrammeled affirmation of religious belief" existed in Canada from its inception.[6]

As so often happens in jurisprudence, a trenchant dissenting opinion, by Mr. Justice Cartright, laid the groundwork for a reversal. In his dissent Cartright wrote:

[T]he purpose and the effect of the Lord's Day Act are to compel, under the penal sanctions of the criminal law, the observance of Sunday as a religious holy day by all the inhabitants of Canada; that this is an infringement of religious freedom I do not doubt. In my opinion a law which compels a course of conduct, whether positive or negative, for a purely religious purpose infringes the freedom of religion.[7]

After the 1982 Canadian Charter of Rights and Freedoms was promulgated, new challenges to Sunday closing legislation were inevitable. A case from Alberta set the stage for an important Supreme Court ruling in 1985. A retail company called Big M Drug Mart Ltd. was acquitted of unlawfully carrying on the sale of goods on Sunday.[8] The Alberta court held that the Lord's Day Act infringed on the freedom of religion now guaranteed by the Canadian Charter of Rights and Freedoms. The Alberta Court of Appeals agreed in 1984.[9] Still, the Attorney-General of Alberta appealed to the Supreme Court of Canada.

The case, *Regina* v. *Big M Drug Mart Ltd.*, was decided on April 24, 1985. The Supreme Court dismissed the appeal and agreed that "in providing for the compulsory observance of the religious institution of the Sabbath (Sunday), the act thereof does infringe on the guarantee of freedom of conscience and religion in Section 2(a) of the Canadian Charter of Rights and Freedoms. Therefore, the Lord's Day Act has no force or effect."[10]

A year before, the Ontario Court of Appeal issued a complex ruling in a challenge to that province's Sunday closing statute. In *Re Regina and Video Flicks Ltd. et al.*[11] the Court held that the effect of the Ontario law for those who worshiped on a day other than Sunday was discriminatory; for others, it was not. The justices sharply distinguished between "those who close their business on a day other than Sunday because it is required as part of their Sabbath observance, and those who do not."[12] Summarizing the decision, the *Canadian Rights Reporter* said:

> The appellants fall into two categories: those who close their business on a day other than Sunday because it is required as part of their Sabbath observance, and those who do not. The Act does not infringe the freedom of conscience or religion of the appellants in the latter category. However, for those appellants who do sincerely observe a day other than Sunday as the Sabbath, the act is a major inducement to work on that day. To be forced to close on two days in a week when competitors can remain open for six days makes observance of one's Sabbath financially onerous. For those appellants the

act has the effect of infringing freedom of religion even though it was enacted for a secular purpose.[13]

The *Canadian Rights Reporter* also acknowledged that the Ontario court had enunciated an important principle of religious expression:

> Freedom of religion as guaranteed by the Charter goes beyond the ability to hold certain beliefs without coercion and restraint and entails more than the ability to profess those beliefs openly. It also includes the right to observe the essential practices demanded by the tenets of one's religion. Freedom of conscience does not mean the mere decision of an individual on any particular occasion to act or not act in a certain way. The behavior in question has to be based upon a set of beliefs by which the individual feels bound to conduct most, if not all, of his actions. A law infringes freedom of religion if it makes it more difficult and costly to practice one's religion.[14]

But in 1986 the Supreme Court of Canada moved back a bit from its expansive prior ruling in a case involving four Ontario retailers who knowingly violated the Retail Business Holidays Act of 1980. The Court majority held that this legislation was enacted with the intent of providing uniform holidays to retail workers, and was not designed to promote Christianity. Any indirect limitations on religious practice resulting from the act did not render it unconstitutional.

The Court denied that "every burden on religious practice infringes the freedom of religion."[15] Continuing, the Court said, "The Constitution shelters individuals and groups only to the extent that religious beliefs or conduct might reasonably or actually be threatened. Legislative or administrative action which increases the cost of practicing or otherwise manifesting religious beliefs is not prohibited if the burden is trivial or insubstantial."[16]

However, the Court held that "the freedom of religion of Saturday-observing retailers is abridged by the Retail Business Holiday Act. . . . The competitive disadvantage experienced by nonexempt Saturday-observing retailers as a result of the act cannot be characterized as insubstantial or trivial. The act also imposes a burden on Saturday-observing consumers in that it circumscribes their ability to go shopping or seek professional services on Sunday."[17]

The Court suggested that legislatures should "attempt to alleviate the effects of those laws on Saturday observers,"[18] and should weigh freedom of religion as an interest along with the interests of those who deserve "a common pause day."[19]

As a practical matter, Sunday shopping is widespread throughout Canada. In 1991 store owners in Ontario opened on Sundays in defiance of the law, or, shall we say, extended the four allowable Sundays before Christmas indefinitely. In an increasingly multicultural and secular society, laws attempting to restrict personal choice for allegedly religious reasons are virtually unenforceable.

7

Religious Rights of Employees

The accommodation of the religious needs of employees in the workplace constitutes an important subsection of church-state law in Canada as well as in the United States. In this regard Canada's Charter has been invoked as a fundamental guarantor of religious free exercise and in preventing employees from being discharged when they seek to practice the dictates of their religious faith.

Beginning in 1985 the Supreme Court of Canada has strengthened the religious rights of employees in three major cases. Karnik Doukmetzian, general counsel of the Seventh-day Adventist Church in Canada, believes that these rulings have substantially advanced religious freedom in Canada. He writes,

Starting with *O'Malley* v. *Simpson Sears*,[1] *Central Alberta Dairy Pool*,[2] and concluding with *Renaud* v. *Central Okanagan School*

District,[3] the Supreme Court of Canada has conclusively stated that the religious beliefs of employees must be accommodated by both the employer and labor union. The issue before the Supreme Court in each instance has been the scope and content of an employer's duty to accommodate the religious beliefs of employees, and in the last case whether that is a corresponding duty to be shared by the trade union. The Court developed the duty as it related to employers in the first two decisions and culminated with the *Renaud* decision extending that duty to the trade union. The Court accepted the proposition that accommodation in the workplace is a multiparty inquiry. . . . More than mere negligible effort by the employer is required to satisfy the duty to accommodate. More than minor inconvenience must be shown before the complainant's right to accommodation can be defeated. The employer must establish that actual interference with the rights of other employees, which is not trivial but substantial, will result from the adoption of the accommodating measures. Minor interference or inconvenience is the price to be paid for religious freedom in a multicultural society.[4]

8

Free Exercise of Religion

While Canada lacks a constitutional guarantee of free exercise, as is found in the religion clauses of the U.S. Constitution's First Amendment, the Dominion has always implicitly recognized the inherent right of individuals to freedom of conscience in religious matters. Even before confederation, the legislature of the United Canadas guaranteed "the free exercise and enjoyment of religious profession and worship, without discrimination or preference" and also affirmed that "the recognition of legal equality among all religious denominations is an admitted principle of colonial legislation."[1]

Scholars and jurists have argued that this principle is indeed imbedded in and vital to the Canadian experience. In a 1953 case involving the Jehovah's Witnesses' clash with authorities in the province of Quebec, the Canadian Supreme Court's Justice Rand expressed this view:

From 1760, therefore, to the present moment religious freedom has, in our legal system, been recognized as a principle of fundamental character; and although we have nothing in the nature of an established church, that the untrammeled affirmations of religious beliefs and its propagation, personal or institutional, remain as of the greatest constitutional significance throughout the Dominion is unquestionable.[2]

In 1960 the Canadian Bill of Rights was promulgated. Its application was limited to federal legislation and was broadly concerned with civil liberties in general. Karnik Doukmetzian writes:

Notwithstanding the apparent lack of legislative codification of civil rights, understanding and accommodation have been an accepted fact in Canada. Religion has been particularly centered out for recognition by the courts which have established as a part of Canadian jurisprudence that no individual should suffer "civil disabilities" because of their religious beliefs or be forced to subscribe to the tenets of any one religion against their will.[3]

Finally, this judicial tradition was codified in the Canadian Charter of Rights and Freedoms, a part of the Constitution Act, 1982. The first "fundamental freedom" guaranteed to "everyone in Canada" in Section 2a is "freedom of conscience and religion."

As we have seen, the Canadian Supreme Court's decisions regarding Sunday closing statutes became occasions for expositions of the meaning and matter of the nation's new Charter. In *Regina* v. *Big M Drug Mart Ltd.* the Court noted, "The essence of the concept of freedom of religion is the right to entertain such religious beliefs as a person chooses, the right to declare religious beliefs openly and without fear of hindrance or reprisal, and the right to manifest religious belief by worship and practice or by teaching and dissemination."[4]

The concept of a Bill of Rights as a defense against majoritarian abuse was also explored in the *Big M* case. The majority decision stated unequivocally, "What may appear good and true to a majoritarian religious group, or to the state acting at their behest, may not, for religious reasons, be imposed upon citizens who take a contrary view. The Charter safeguards religious minorities from the threat of 'the tyranny of the majority.' "[5]

The libertarian impulse underlying freedom of conscience was affirmed in the following discussion in the same ruling:

It should also be noted that an emphasis on individual conscience and individual judgment lies at the heart of our democratic political tradition. The ability of each citizen to make free and informed decisions is the absolute prerequisite for the legitimacy, acceptability, and efficacy of our system of self-government. . . . Viewed in this context, the purpose of freedom of conscience and religion becomes clear. The values that underlie our political and philosophic traditions demand that every individual be free to hold and to manifest whatever beliefs and opinions his or her conscience dictates, provided inter alia only that such manifestations do not injure his or her neighbors or their parallel rights to hold and manifest beliefs and opinions of their own. Religious belief and practice are historically prototypical and, in many ways, paradigmatic of conscientiously held beliefs and manifestations and are therefore protected by the Charter. Equally protected, and for the same reasons, are expressions and manifestations of religious nonbelief and refusals to participate in religious practice.[6]

9

Religious Establishment

While Canada's Charter lacks a ban on religious establishment, there is, according to many scholars, a kind of
unwritten ban on the concept. John Moir, in his study of
church-state relations in preconfederation Canada, argues:

> Canadians in fact assume the presence of an unwritten sepa-
> ration of church and state, without denying an essential con-
> nection between religious principles and national life or the
> right of the churches to speak out on matters of public impor-
> tance. This ill-defined—and difficult to define—relationship
> is peculiarly Canadian. It is an attitude of mind accepted and
> understood by Canadians but equally incomprehensible as a
> compromise to citizens of either the United States or the
> British Isles.[1]

On the other hand, it is arguable that Canada's Charter implies a dependence upon and an appreciation of religion, since both the Canadian Bill of Rights and the Charter of Rights and Freedoms affirm that the nation "is founded upon principles that acknowledge and recognize the supremacy of God." This was acknowledged by the Federal Court of Canada in a 1984 case involving religious education. The Court declared:

> It is apparent that both the advancement of education and the advancement of religion are firmly and favorably rooted in the public policy of our law. Moreover, it is not stretching matters to say that even in the modern, secular age the advancement of religion is rooted in our law and our Constitution. That policy is readily discernible in the declaratory preambles of the Canadian Bill of Rights and the Canadian Charter of Rights and Freedoms. . . . That is not to say that our country is even remotely similar to . . . theocrac[ies] such as have been established in past ages and in the present day in some countries. Far from it. We do not have any state church or state religion. Those Canadians who profess atheism, agnosticism, or the philosophy of secularism are just as secure in their civil rights and freedoms as are those who profess religion. So it is that while Canada may aptly be characterized as a secular state, yet being declared by both Parliament and the Constitution to be founded upon principles which recognize "the supremacy of God," it cannot be said that our public policy is entirely neutral in terms of the advancement of religion.[2]

When all the ramifications are considered, Canada's record of preserving religious freedom is an admirable one. Doukmetzian concludes:

There is no danger in Canada that any government would wish to establish an official state church, though less obvious favoritism remains a problem. There was a time when religion was more often the focus of attention. Canadian society has become more pluralistic, with a wide range of religious practices and beliefs. This, coupled with a relatively secular age, has resulted in religion playing less of a part in public life than it once did. Now, it is one concern among many. The lack of legal precedent to deal with particular situations has allowed our courts the opportunity to develop principles that are consistent with contemporary views about religion, resulting in very understanding and accommodating pronouncements in harmony with the multicultural, multifaceted nature of our society.[3]

10

Religion, Politics, and Moral Issues

Canada's relatively conservative and church-oriented society began to change dramatically in the 1960s. Statutory restrictions on birth control and divorce faced overhaul in the legislative machinery.

In 1966 the House of Commons Standing Committee on Health and Welfare held public hearings to determine whether the legal prohibition on contraception, found in Article 150 of the Criminal Code, should be abolished. In October the Canadian Catholic bishops submitted their opinion, saying in effect that they would not oppose changes in the existing laws. "That which the church teaches to be morally reprehensible should not necessarily be considered as indictable by the criminal code of a country,"[1] they asserted. Furthermore, says Michael W. Cuneo, a sociologist of religion, "The bishops asserted that Catholic legislators are not bound to vote only for laws that are in conformity with the teachings of the church."[2] They stated boldly, "Catholic legislators should not stand idly by waiting for the church to tell them what to do in the political order."[3]

Even on divorce law reform the bishops adopted a moderate stance. A Special Joint Committee of the Senate and House tackled the divorce issue in 1967. The bishops' statement again drew a distinction between civil law and church doctrine:

> Canada is a country of many religious beliefs. Since other citizens, desiring as we do the promotion of the common good, believe that it is less injurious to the individual and to society that divorce be permitted in certain circumstances, we would not object to some revision of Canadian divorce laws that is truly directed to advancing the common good of civil society.[4]

Cuneo interprets the bishops' posture as evidence of their desire to apply the Second Vatican Council's directives to the exigencies of Canadian life. "The bishops clearly had no desire to puncture this mood of ecumenical freshness by resurrecting the specter of triumphalism, and thus their statements on contraceptives and divorce were marked by deferential caution," he says.[5]

The campaign for abortion law liberalization put the bishops in a quandary. Their decision to oppose abortion reform in a relatively civil way has provoked a backlash from conservative, traditionalist Catholics, but has also reawakened fears by liberals in all religious communities about increased religious intrusion in politics. Cuneo writes, "Whereas the American bishops responded to *Roe* v. *Wade* with uninhibited activism, and in fact greatly facilitated the development of an organized antiabortion front, the Canadian bishops have left the movement entirely to its own devices."[6]

Cuneo studied the phenomenon of the antiabortion movement in Canada and found that it developed wholly on its own by disaffected lay people he calls "Revivalist Catholics." He argues:

> The Canadian pro-life (or antiabortion) movement is fraught with paradox. It is a vehicle of both unity and disunity, a symbol of both common and divergent purpose for Canadian Roman Catholicism. The movement is at once a shibboleth of Catholic identity and a fulcrum of internal conflict for the Canadian church. It is overwhelmingly Roman Catholic in composition and yet scorned by Canadian Catholic elites and scarcely tolerated by most bishops. Moreover, despite its quintessential Catholicity, many movement activists regard the institutional Canadian church with unconcealed contempt.[7]

The movement eventually attracted the kind of conservative Catholic-evangelical Protestant alliance found on this issue in the United States. Cuneo continues:

> For its first decade of existence the movement was overwhelmingly Roman Catholic in composition. The thickly Catholic atmosphere of right-to-life groups and an ingrained theological suspicion of political involvement discouraged most Protestant evangelicals from translating their antiabortion sentiments into activism. By about 1977, however, perhaps emboldened by the dramatic entrance of American evangelicalism into the political theater, more Canadian evangelicals set aside theological scruples and joined the antiabortion fray. Some of these started independent pro-life groups, such as Christians Concerned for Life (Calgary), some operated crisis pregnancy centers, and others joined already established right-to-life groups. Evangelicals-turned-

activist belonged to smaller denominations such as the Christian and Missionary Alliance, the Pentecostal Assemblies of Canada, the Convention and Fellowship Baptist churches, and the Canadian Reformed Church. The last denomination, not evangelical in the strict sense, would in future years play a role in the movement far disproportionate to its size or influence within the spectrum of Canadian Protestantism. In addition, the Christian Action Council, a consortium of anti-abortion evangelicals which originated in the United States, would, by the late 1970s, make a modest dent in the movement. And finally, Choose Life Canada, an antiabortion out-growth of evangelical preacher Ken Campbell's Renaissance Canada ministry, would be launched in 1985 with the purpose of bringing more evangelicals into the pro-life fold.[8]

Cuneo argues that the antiabortion lobby "retained its distinctly Catholic stamp" because "Canadian evangelicalism is a distinctly minority phenomenon with an underdeveloped tradition of social engagement."[9]

This is largely where the movement exists today, with little real chance of overturning Canada's abortion laws. Says Cuneo:

It is extremely unlikely that the bishops would force a show-down with members of the Canadian laity over the abortion issue. Such a showdown would potentially reveal that many, and perhaps most, Canadian Catholics have ceased to regard the institutional church as a source of absolute moral authority. Indeed, *Humanae Vitae* proved perhaps better than any-thing else that Canadian Catholics, far from looking to the hierarchy for moral directives, practice their religion as a pri-vate affair. Any attempt by the Canadian hierarchy to make adherence to the traditional teaching against abortion a nec-essary condition of Catholic belonging would just as likely be greeted by lay indifference and thereby further amplify the diminished control exercised by the bishops over the Canadian church.[10]

What the abortion issue has done is to fragment Catholicism. As Cuneo concludes:

> Whereas Revivalists regard opposition to abortion as the touchstone of genuine faith, Canadian Catholic elites, including most bishops, priests, and nuns, treat the issue with a circumspection bordering on avoidance. Although Catholic elites are generally uncomfortable with the trend toward greater abortion freedom, the pro-life cause is beyond the pale of the progressive ecumenism to which they are committed.[11]

On other social issues, Canada's Catholic bishops have sharply criticized many of the economic inequities and political institutions of their society. So have the mainline Protestant groups, whose positions on public policy issues resemble those of their U.S. coreligionists. Canada's religious groups have far less influence on public policy and have much weaker and more informal lobbies in Ottawa and the provincial capitals than do their counterparts in the United States.

Nearly thirty thousand Canadians voted for the new Christian Heritage party (CHP) in the 59 ridings (constituencies) which the fundamentalist group contested in the October 25, 1993 elections. Its total vote of 29,698 represented only 1.1 percent of the vote cast in those parliamentary constituencies. Since it fielded no candidates in four-fifths of Canada's 295 ridings, its impact is minuscule.

The CHP concentrated its efforts in rural, Protestant, English-speaking areas. Only two of its candidates ran in Quebec, the most Catholic and French-speaking province. The CHP ran no candidate in other Francophone strongholds in New Brunswick or Ontario, nor did it make much of an effort in liberal, multicultural cities like Toronto, Vancouver, and Montreal.

In only five ridings did the CHP exceed 2 percent of the vote. Its best showing (3.8 percent) came in Lambton-Middlesex in Ontario, followed by 3.2 percent in Elgin-Norfolk, also in Ontario. The CHP candidate topped 2 percent in Medicine Hat in rural Alberta and in Fraser Valley East and Skeena in British Columbia, the most secular province. Three of these five ridings elected the Reform party candidate, Canada's new right-wing party which won fifty-two seats in western Canada and replaced the Progressive Conservatives as the main opposition group outside of Quebec. The Liberal party won a landslide nationally, especially in Ontario, and holds 177 of the 295 seats.

An unusual number of CHP candidates were of Dutch ancestry, e.g., Rien Van Den Enden in Hamilton-Wentworth and Sid Vander Heide in Perth.

Historically, Canada's Liberals received the majority of Catholic votes, from both French and English speakers, while the Conservatives were the Protestant party, especially in Ontario and the Maritime Provinces. But Canada has changed dramatically since World War II. Many Catholics are of Italian, Portuguese, Hungarian, and Ukrainian ancestry, and dozens of other ethnic groups add to the mosaic of Canadian Catholicism. Many liberal Protestants long ago deserted the Conservatives for the Liberals or New Democrats. On the other hand, many Catholics have voted Conservative, and the last Conservative Prime Minister, Brian Mulroney, is a Quebec Catholic of Irish descent. Some of this realignment came in Ontario, where the Conservative party broke with its Scottish-flavored Orange Protestant heritage and supported generous funding for Catholic schools—an issue which gains some voters and loses others.

The Reform party, which came out of nowhere to replace the Progressive Conservatives as English Canada's primary opposition party in the 1993 election, is led by a staunch evangelical, Preston Manning. Manning, who attends an evangelical Alliance Church in Calgary, is the son of a longtime political firebrand, Ernest Manning, who served as Alberta's premier for many years. The elder Manning was also a radio evangelist during his years as the province's chief executive, which would have been considered inappropriate, if not bizarre and possibly unconstitutional, in the United States. Manning represented the Social Credit party, a kind of "funny money" neopopulist conservative group somewhat akin to the Greenback party that developed in the western part of the United States in the late nineteenth century. So both Mannings have their origins in western protest politics and in fundamentalist Protestantism.

The Reform party's platform avoided church-state issues, but Preston Manning's personal opposition to abortion was notable, even though he said he would not attempt to legislate those views. The party won all of its fifty-two seats in English-speaking Protestant areas, and did not even contest Quebec. It could be considered, at least indirectly, a religious-based political party if it appeals to only one part of the religious community in a religiously pluralistic society such as Canada.

In one area Canada is clearly ahead of the United States. Religious affiliation has never played a key role in the selection of the prime minister, as has the unwritten Protestant-only rule for the presidency in the United States (broken only once in two centuries). Canadians elected a Catholic prime minister in 1896, a full sixty-four years before the United States elected John F. Kennedy. Most recent prime ministers, including Pierre Trudeau, Brian Mulroney, and the incumbent, Jean Chrétien, have been Roman Catholic, and their elections did not result in furor or hysteria.

Canadian legislators voted unanimously in February of 1994 to revise the daily prayer that begins each session of the federal Parliament in Ottawa. The new prayer substitutes "Almighty God" for Jesus Christ and also deletes references to Britain's royal family. (The legislators still pray for Queen Elizabeth, "our sovereign.")

Observers attribute the change to Canada's multicultural, multireligious character. While the majority of Canadians adhere to the Christian faith, at least nominally, more than 22 percent are members of other—or no—formal religious traditions.

The new prayer, which is brief and employs modern language, was praised as "graceful, appropriate, and more than just an accommodation for political correctness" by the Toronto *Star*.

Peter Milliken, a Liberal member of the parliament who headed the committee drafting the new prayer said it was "extremely fair and a good compromise." Louis Plamondon, a leader of the Bloc Québécois, the party advocating the secession of Quebec from Canada, said he was irked by the continued reference to the queen but supported the overall revision.

Preston Manning, leader of the conservative Reform party and an evangelical on religion, called the final version acceptable. He said it was an improvement on an earlier proposal which deleted references to any supreme being.

The first Sikh member of Canada's House of Commons, Gurbax Malhi, endorsed the change, saying, "This prayer respects everybody."

Not everyone was so sanguine. Most representatives of Canada's new right-wing Reform party, who are mostly conservative Protestants, expressed vocal dismay. Myron Thompson of Wild Rose, Alberta, said the prayer betrays Canada's Christian moorings. "This country was founded on the principles and values of the Christian faith and the Christian faith is based on the life of Jesus Christ. Canada should not change and get away from the founding principles and values that this country was built on," he remarked. Thompson, who favored retention of the florid, Victorian-style prayer written in 1877, said he was not concerned about the religious pluralism in parliament or in the country. One of the two remaining Conservative party members, Elsie Wayne of Saint John, New Brunswick, said she would have favored a moment of silence for non-Christians after the formal, spoken Christian-oriented prayer.

The New Version of the Prayer

Almighty God, we give thanks for the great blessings which have been bestowed on Canada and its citizens, including the gifts of freedom, opportunity, and peace that we enjoy.

We pray for our sovereign, Queen Elizabeth, and the governor-general.

Guide us in our deliberations as Members of Parliament and strengthen us in our awareness of our duties and responsibilities as members.

Grant us wisdom, knowledge, and understanding to preserve the blessings of this country for the benefit of all and to make good laws and wise decisions.

The Old Version

O Lord our heavenly Father, high and mighty, King of kings, Lord of lords, the only Ruler of princes, who dost from thy throne behold all the dwellers upon earth: Most heartily we beseech thee with thy favor to behold our most gracious sovereign lady, Queen Elizabeth; and so replenish her with the grace of thy Holy Spirit that she may always incline to thy will and walk in thy way: Endue her plenteously with heavenly gifts; grant her in health and wealth long to live; strengthen her that she may vanquish and overcome all her enemies; and finally, after this life, she may attain everlasting joy and felicity; through Jesus Christ our Lord—Amen.

Almighty God, the fountain of goodness, we humbly beseech thee to bless Elizabeth the Queen Mother; Prince Philip, Duke of Edinburgh; Charles, Prince of Wales; and all the royal family: Endue them with the Holy Spirit; enrich them with thy heavenly grace; prosper them with all happiness; and bring them to thine everlasting kingdom; through Jesus Christ our Lord—Amen.

Most gracious God, we humbly beseech thee, as for the United Kingdom, Canada, and Her Majesty's other realms and territories, so especially for Canada, and herein more particularly for the governor-general, the Senate, and the House of Commons, in their legislative capacity at this time assembled; that thou wouldst be pleased to direct and prosper all their consultations, to the advancement of their glory, the safety, honor, and welfare of our sovereign and her realms and territories, that all things may be so ordered and settled by their endeavors, upon the best and surest foundations, that peace and happiness, truth and justice, religion and piety, may be established among us for all generations. These, and all other necessaries for them, and for us, we humbly beg in thy name.

11

Divorce and Other Matters

Divorce is a common phenomenon of life in virtually all nations, including Canada. The Canadian divorce rate has been declining, from 355.1 divorces per 100,000 population in 1987 to 294.0 in 1990, a reduction of almost 20 percent. Alberta, the Yukon, British Columbia, and Quebec have higher rates than the rest of the nation. Newfoundland and the Northwest Territories have the lowest rates. Prince Edward Island, New Brunswick, and Saskatchewan are below average. Average rates are found in Nova Scotia, Ontario, and Manitoba.

In terms of directional change, the divorce rate has declined most in Ontario, Manitoba, British Columbia, and the Yukon. The rate is virtually unchanged in Newfoundland, and the divorce rate has actually increased in Quebec and Prince Edward Island. There seems to be some correlation between divorce and religious affiliation, as in the United States, where strongly Roman Catholic states in the Northeast have consistently lower divorce rates. (See Table 5.)

Table 5

Divorce Rate by Province—1990

Province	Divorces Per 100,000 Population
Alberta	343.5
Yukon	311.5
British Columbia	310. 9
Quebec	301.6
Ontario	296.6
Nova Scotia	270.7
Manitoba	252.8
Saskatchewan	235.3
New Brunswick	234.1
Prince Edward Island	211.7
Newfoundland	175.6
Northwest Territories	170.4
NATION	294. 0

Source: *Statistics Canada*

Church Tax Exemptions

Canadian municipalities generally grant exemptions from taxation for churches and church-related activities, and for those portions of church-owned businesses that are used exclusively for religious purposes. These decisions are made by cities, counties, or other municipalities. They are not decided at the federal or provincial levels.

Clergy and full-time church administrative personnel

receive a clergy housing (manse) allowance, which reduces the taxable income of those who are eligible.

Charitable Contribution Deductions

Contributions made to churches and other charities are deductible from Canada's federal income tax. A graduated system is used, which is computed as a tax credit. Proof of contributions is required. The same rules apply to provincial income taxes.

Chaplains

Canada provides chaplains and religious ministration programs to its armed forces members and their dependents. Canada has voluntary participation in its military. The most recent data from the Defense Ministry show 196 Protestant and 136 Catholic chaplains.

12

Canada and the United States: A Summary Comparison

Comparisons between the religious cultures of Canada and the United States are instructive. There are some basic similarities. Both countries have had a dominant British Protestant heritage, at least in the early centuries of national historical development. The upper classes and the Establishment continued to reflect this orientation long after both nations had become more pluralistic. Owing to its French heritage, Canada has always had a larger Catholic presence, and its influence has, as in the United States, increased in the twentieth century. In both nations all religious bodies more or less accepted British political norms and a democratic constitutionalism in government and, to some extent, in the governing apparatus of the churches.

In both nations religion tended to play a conservative, individualistic role, concentrating on family values, religious education, and personal relationships, even though social welfare and charitable enterprises were prominent in church structures. The dominant religious groups tended to set the moral norms and defined community values. They were forces of stability and support for the presuppositions and values of society. They reinforced loyalty to the government. Both in Canada and the United States, religious bodies tended to support national foreign policies. In both nations Protestantism tended more toward the evangelical side of the spectrum, at least until early in the twentieth century. Both nations had an overwhelming Christian numerical superiority, though communities of Jews added to the mosaic, especially in urban areas.

But there are numerous differences in religious styles and life contexts which define religious life. Perhaps most basic is the underlying conservatism of Canadian history in comparison with the ever-changing, almost revolutionary nature of U.S. society. The United States was born in revolution against Britain; Canada represented a settlement of loyalty toward the Crown. The United States celebrates its differentness, its breaking away from the Old World in political and, as a consequence, church-state relationships. Canada was preoccupied with preserving its Anglo-French heritage, and resisted the kind of multicultural, diffuse society that characterized the United States. (Canada has followed suit to some extent since World War II.) As historian Mark Noll explains it, "Where Americans laud the ideals of their Revolutionary heritage, Canadians celebrate the virtues of loyalism. . . . Canada has always lacked the sort of compelling myths that fuel American ideology."[1] Canadians, says Noll, "chose not the way of revolution and independence but of loyalism and peaceful change."[2]

This may be why Canada has avoided civil war and the kind of political violence that has taken the lives of four U.S. presidents. Canada's orderly society has many admirable qualities. Notable are its medical care system and its relatively low crime rate. Americans have much to learn from the Canadian pattern. Writing in *Foreign Affairs,* Conrad Black made this insightful comparison:

> Canada's less complex sociology and strict gun control rules have undoubtedly made Canada a more peaceable country than its neighbor. American per capita murder rates are four times Canada's, and the United States has nearly three times as many imprisoned people per capita as Canada. . . . Canada has adopted a notion of public policy more like the protective model found in climatically and ethnically similar Scandinavian countries, rather than the individualism of the more temperate and diverse United States.[3]

Canadians could profit from the United States's experience in church-state relationships. A firm separation between the institutions of church and state and a commitment to free, publicly financed education without entangling alliances between education and religion are policies which guarantee the preservation of religious liberty and freedom of conscience at a maximum level.

Notes

Chapter 1

1. William A. DeGregorio, *The Complete Book of U.S. Presidents* (New York: Dembner, 1991), p. 5.

2. Susan E. Merritt, *Her Story: Women from Canada's Past* (St. Catharines, Ontario: Vanwell Publishing, Ltd., 1994), p. 77.

3. Charles Trueheart, "Canada's Harbors of Hope," *Washington Post*, February 12, 1995, p. E1.

4. Mark Lightbody and Tom Smallman, *Canada* (Berkeley, Calif.: Lonely Planet Publications, 1994), p. 33.

5. Lightbody and Smallman, *Canada*, p. 606.

6. Michael Harris, *Unholy Orders: Tragedy at Mount Cashel* (New York: Viking, 1990), pp. 366–67.

7. Ibid., p. 19.

8. Ibid., p. 369.

9. Ibid.

129

10. Ibid., p. xxv.

11. Ibid. p. xxi.

12. Ibid., p. xxiii.

13. Ibid., pp. xxi-xxii.

14. Lightbody and Smallman, *Canada,* p. 219.

15. Ibid., p. 173.

16. Mark A. Noll, *A History of Christianity in the United States and Canada* (Grand Rapids, Mich.: William B. Eerdmans Publishing Co., 1992), p. 126.

17. Ibid., p. 24.

18. Kenneth McNaught, *The Penguin History of Canada* (Toronto: Penguin Books Canada, Ltd., 1988), p. 161.

19. Noll, *A History of Christianity,* p. 260.

20. John A. Dickinson and Brian Young, *A Short History of Quebec* (Toronto: Copp Clarke Pitman, Ltd., 1993), p. 179.

21. Ibid., p. 236.

22. Ibid., p. 237.

23. Ibid., p. 236.

24. Ibid.

25. Ibid., p. 252.

26. Ibid., p. 286.

27. Ibid., p. 285.

28. Ibid.

29. Quoted in McNaught, *The Penguin History of Canada,* p. 273.

30. Noll, *A History of Christianity,* p. 450.

31. Peter Nichols, *The Pope's Divisions: The Roman Catholic Church Today* (New York: Holt, Rinehart & Winston, 1981), pp. 334, 335.

32. Ibid., p. 336.

33. Dickinson and Young, *A Short History of Quebec,* p. 323.

34. Ibid., p. 327.

35. Mordecai Richler, *Oh Canada! Oh Quebec!* (New York: Penguin, 1992), pp. 152, 181.

36. *Montreal Gazette,* November 14 and 15, 1990.

37. Richler, *Oh Canada!* pp. 59–77.

38. Quoted in Richler, *Oh Canada!* p. 253.

39. *Toronto Globe and Mail,* September 21, 1991.

40. Richler, *Oh Canada!* p. 254.

41. Ibid., p. 211.

42. Ibid., p. 201.

Chapter 2

1. Bernard J. Shapiro, *Report of the Commission in Private Schools in Ontario* (Toronto: October 1985).

2. For a history of this conflict, see Robert M. Stamp, *The Historical Background to Separate Schools in Ontario* (Toronto: Ontario Government Publication Centre, 1985).

3. Ontario, *Hansard* 1843–1845.

4. Carl J. Matthews, "In Toronto Catholic Schools are Public," *Momentum* (February 1990): 28.

5. "Canadian Holy War Over Parochiaid Erupts in Violence," *Church & State* 44 (October 1991): 12.

6. Matthews, *Momentum,* p. 28.

7. Ibid., pp. 26–28.

8. Ibid., p. 28.

9. Andrew Duffy, "Religious Schools Get Hearing," *Toronto Star,* February 3, 1995.

10. Ibid.

11. Ibid.

12. Ibid.

13. Matthews, *Momentum,* p. 26.

14. Ibid., p. 28.

15. *Toronto Star,* September 7, 1994.

16. Rita Daly, "Teacher's Win Called Threat to Catholic Education," *Toronto Star,* September 11, 1994.

17. Sue-Ann Levy, "Barred Teacher Gets Her Job Back," *Toronto Sun,* September 14, 1994.

18. Douglas Todd, Religious News Service, June 3, 1994.

19. Andrew Duffy, "Metro Board Opposes Funds to Support Religious Schools," *Toronto Star*, September 9, 1993. See also Gissela Ruebsaat, *The First Freedom: Freedom of Conscience and Religion in Canada*, available from Conscience Canada, Inc. in Victoria, British Columbia.

20. Renton H. Patterson, *Not Carved in Stone: Public Funding of Separate Schools in Ontario* (Burnstown, Ontario: General Store Publishing House, 1992), p. 31.

21. Ibid., p. 47.

22. Paul Pfalzner, "Religion in Canadian Public School Systems," *Humanist in Canada* 21 (Winter 1988): 21.

23. Charles L. Glenn, *Choice of Schools in Six Nations* (Washington, D.C.: U.S. Government Printing Office, 1989), p. 153.

24. Matthews, *Momentum*, p. 26.

25. Glenn, *Choice of Schools*, p. 162.

26. Ibid.

27. Ibid., p. 163.

28. Ibid., p. 166.

29. André Picard, "Montreal Principal Denounced for Ousting Teen in Islamic Garb," *Toronto Globe and Mail*, September 10, 1994.

30. *National and International Religion Report* 8, August 8, 1994, p. 8.

31. Glenn, *Choice of Schools*, p. 178.

32. Ibid., p. 178.

33. Ibid., pp. 174–75.

34. Ibid., p. 177.

35. Ibid., p. 173.

36. Ibid., p. 171.

37. See "Newfoundland's Patchwork," *Friends of Public Education in Ontario Newsletter* 6 (February 1990).

38. "Vote on Newfoundland Church Schools Decried," *Toronto Globe and Mail*, August 15, 1987.

39. Quoted in Patterson, *Not Carved in Stone*, p. 51.

40. Glenn, *Choice of Schools*, p. 160.

41. Ibid.

42. "Newfoundland Vows to Scrap Church-run Schooling," *Toronto Star*, August 20, 1994.

43. Matthews, *Momentum,* p. 26.

44. John J. Bergen, "The Private School Movement in Canada," *Education Canada,* Summer 1981.

45. Glenn, *Choice of Schools,* p. 161.

Chapter 3

1. Noll, *A History of Christianity in the United States and Canada,* p. 470.

2. Ibid., p. 548.

3. Ibid., pp. 476–77.

4. Ibid., p. 477.

5. Ibid., p. 478.

6. Ibid., p. 549.

7. Ibid., p. 548.

8. Ibid., p. 550.

Chapter 4

1. Reginald W. Bibby, *Fragmented Gods: The Poverty and Potential of Religion in Canada* (Toronto: Stoddart Publishing Co. Ltd., 1990 paperback ed.), p. 5.

2. Ibid., p. 4.

3. Ibid., p. 11.

4. Ibid., p. 20.

5. Ibid., p. 13.

6. Ibid., p. 32.

7. Ibid., p. 5.

8. Ibid., p. 164.

9. Ibid., pp. 28–29.

10. Ibid., p. 23.

11. Ibid., p. 82.

12. Ibid., p. 89.

13. Allan Gregg and Michael Posner, *The Big Picture: What Cana-*

dians Think About Almost Everything (Toronto: Macfarlane, Walter and Ross, 1990), p. 61.

14. Ibid., p. 67.

15. Ibid., p. 64.

16. Ibid., p. 65.

Chapter 5

1. Shelagh Day and Stan Persky, eds., *The Supreme Court of Canada Decision on Abortion* (Vancouver: New Star Books, 1988), p. 162.

2. Ibid., pp. 162–63.

3. Ibid., p. 8.

4. Ibid., p. 13.

5. Ibid., pp. 13–18.

6. Ibid., p. 21.

7. Anne Swardson, "Canada Abortion Doctor Says Battle Is Won," *Washington Post*, October 16, 1994.

8. Ibid.

9. Day and Persky, *The Supreme Court*, p. 205. Also see Arlene Tigar McLaren and Angus McLaren, *The Bedroom and the State: The Changing Practices and Politics of Abortion and Contraception in Canada* (Toronto: McClelland and Stewart, 1987).

10. *Statistics Canada*, Cat. 82–219.

Chapter 6

1. *Lord's Day Alliance* v. *A.–G. Man. et al.*, A.C. 384, 43 C.C.C. 185, [1925] 1 D.L.R. 561.

2. *Lord's Day Alliance* v. *A.–G. B. C. et al.*, S.C.R. 497, 123 C.C.C. 81, 30 C.R. 193.

3. *Hodge* v. *The Queen*, 9 App. Cas. 117 (1883).

4. *A.–G. Ont.* v. *Hamilton Street Railway Co.*, A.C. 524, 7 C.C.C. 326, 20. W.R. 672 (1903).

5. *Ouimet* v. *Bazin*, 46 S.C.P. 502, 20 C.C.C. 458, 3 D.L.R. 593 (1912).

6. *Robertson and Rosetanni* v. *The Queen*, S.C.R. 651, 1 C.C.C. 1, 41 C.R. 392 (1963) at 660.

7. Ibid.

8. 5 C.R.R. 281, (1983) 4 W.W.R. 54, 25 Alta. L.R. (2d) 195.

9. 7 C.R.R. 92, 9 C.C.C. (3d) 310, (1984) 1 W.W.R. 625.

10. 13 C.R.R. at 112.

11. 9 C.R.R. 193–236.

12. 9 C.R.R. 195.

13. Ibid.

14. 9 C.R.R. 194.

15. *Edwards Books and Art Ltd. et al.* v. *The Queen*, 28 C.R.R. 3.

16. Ibid.

17. Ibid.

18. 28 C.R.R. at 4.

19. Ibid.

Chapter 7

1. *Ontario Human Rights Commission and O'Malley* v. *Simpson Sears Limited* (1985) 2 S.C.R. 536.

2. *Alberta Human Rights Commission* v. *Central Alberta Dairy Pool* (1990) 2 S.C.R. 489.

3. (1992) 2 S.C.R. 302.

4. Karnik Doukmetzian, "Church-State Relations in Canada," unpublished paper.

Chapter 8

1. This 1851 Act is cited in Doukmetzian, "Church-State Relations in Canada."

2. *Saumaur* v. *The City of Quebec* (1953) 2 S.C.R. 299 at 327.

3. Doukmetzian, pp. 5–6.

4. 13 C.R.R. at 97.

5. 13 C.R.R. at 98.

6. 13 C.R.R. at 105.

Chapter 9

1. John Moir, *Church and State in Canada, 1627–1867*, p. xii.
2. *McBurney* v. *The Queen*, (1984) 84 D. T. C. 6494 (F. C. C.)
3. Doukmetzian, "Church-State Relations in Canada," pp. 17–18.

Chapter 10

1. *Contraception, Divorce, Abortion: Three Statements by Canadian Catholic Conference* (Ottawa: Canadian Catholic Conference, 1968), cited in Michael W. Cuneo, *Catholics Against the Church: Anti-Abortion Protest in Toronto 1969–1985* (Toronto: University of Toronto Press, 1989), p. 233.
2. Cuneo, *Catholics Against the Church*, p. 27.
3. Ibid., p. 233.
4. *Canadian Catholic Conference*, p. 23.
5. Cuneo, *Catholics Against the Church*, p. 30.
6. Ibid., p. 24.
7. Ibid., p. ix.
8. Ibid., pp. 12–13.
9. Ibid.
10. Ibid., pp. 207–208.
11. Ibid., p. 215.

Chapter 12

1. Noll, *A History of Christianity in the United States and Canada*, pp. 545, 546.
2. Ibid., p. 547.
3. Conrad Black, "Canada's Continuing Identity Crisis," *Foreign Affairs* 74 (March/April 1995): 99–115, at 103.

Suggestions for Further Reading

In addition to the books and articles cited in the notes, the following titles are recommended.

Alton, Bruce, ed. *The Abortion Question*. Toronto: Anglican Book Centre, 1983.

Appleblatt, Anthony. "The School Question in the 1929 Saskatchewan Provincial Election." *Canadian Catholic Historical Association: Study Sessions* 43 (1976).

Baum, Gregory, and Duncan Cameron. *Catholics and Canadian Socialism*. Toronto: James Lorimer, 1980.

———. *Ethics and Economics: Canada's Catholic Bishops on the Economic Crisis*. Toronto: James Lorimer, 1984.

Berton, Pierre. *Why We Act Like Canadians*. Toronto: McClelland and Stewart, 1982 (Revised paperback edition, Penguin Books Canada, 1987).

Bothwell, Robert, Ian Drummond, and John English. *Canada 1900–1945.* Toronto: University of Toronto Press, 1987.

———. *Canada Since 1945.* Toronto: University of Toronto Press, 1989.

Brook, Stephen. *Maple Leaf Rag.* New York: Random House, 1987.

Bumsted, J. M. *Interpreting Canada's Past.* Toronto: Oxford University Press, 1993.

Carter, G. Emmet. *The Catholic Public Schools of Quebec.* Toronto: W. J. Gage, 1957.

———. *The Modern Challenge to Religious Education.* New York: William H. Sadlier, 1961.

Clark, S. D. "The Religious Sect in Canadian Politics." In *The Developing Canadian Community,* 131–46. Toronto: University of Toronto Press, 1968.

Clifford, N. K. "His Dominion: A Vision in Crisis." In *Religion and Culture in Canada,* edited by Peter Slater, Canadian Corporation for Studies in Religion, 1977.

Coleman, William D. *The Independence Movement in Quebec 1945–1980.* Toronto: University of Toronto Press, 1984.

Collins, Ann. *The Big Evasion: Abortion, the Issue That Won't Go Away.* Toronto: Lester & Orpen Dennys, 1985.

Creighton, Phyllis, ed. *Abortion: An Issue for Conscience.* Toronto: The Anglican Church of Canada, 1974.

Cuneo, Michael W. *Catholics Against the Church: Anti-Abortion Protest in Toronto, 1969–1985.* Toronto: University of Toronto Press, 1989.

Danylewysz, Marta. *Taking the Veil: An Alternative to Marriage, Motherhood and Spinsterhood in Quebec, 1840–1920.* Toronto: McClelland and Stewart, 1987.

Friesen, Gerald. *The Canadian Prairies: A History.* Toronto: University of Toronto, 1987.

Fry, Earl H. *Canada's Unity Crisis.* New York: Twentieth Century Fund Press, 1992.

Godfrey, Sheldon J., and Judith C. *Search Out the Land: The Jewish Contribution to Civil and Political Equality in Canada.* Montreal: McGill-Queens University Press, 1995.

Grant, John W. *The Church in the Canadian Era.* Toronto: Anasi, 1986.

Graubard, Stephen R., ed. *In Search of Canada.* New Brunswick, N.J.: Transaction Books, 1989.

Guindon, Hubert. *Quebec Society.* Toronto: University of Toronto Press, 1988.

Handy, Robert T. *A History of the Churches in the United States and Canada.* Toronto: University of Toronto Press, 1984.

Higgins, Michael, and Douglas R. Letson. *Portraits of Canadian Catholicism.* Toronto: Griffin House, 1986.

Hoy, Claire. *Bill Davis.* Toronto: Methuen, 1985.

Hughes, Everett C. *French Canada in Transition.* Chicago: University of Chicago Press, 1943.

Jaenen, Cornelius. *The Role of the Church in New France.* Toronto: McGraw-Hill Ryerson, 1976.

Lamont, Lansing. *Breakup: The Coming End of Canada and the Stakes for America.* New York: Norton, 1994.

McBride, Stephen, and John Shields. *Dismantling a Nation: Canada and the New World Order.* Halifax, N.S.: Fernwood, 1993.

McLaughlin, Kenneth M. "Race, Religion and Politics: The Election of 1896 in Canada." University of Toronto, 1974.

McNaught, Kenneth. *The Penguin History of Canada.* Toronto: Penguin Books Canada, Ltd., 1988.

Malcolm, Andrew H. *The Canadians.* New York: St. Martin's, 1985.

Mathews, George. *Quiet Revolution: Quebec's Challenge to Canada.* Toronto: Summerhill Press, 1990.

Miller, J. R. "Anti-Catholic Thought in Victorian Canada." *Canadian Historical Review* 66 (1985).

Morton, Desmond. *A Short History of Canada.* Edmonton: Hurtia, 1983.

Pelrine, Eleanor. *Morgentaler: The Doctor Who Couldn't Turn Away.* Toronto: Gage, 1975.

Sheridan, E. F., ed. *Do Justice! The Social Teaching of the Canadian Catholic Bishops* (1945–1986). Toronto: The Jesuit Centre for Social Faith and Justice, 1987.

Sissons, C. B. *Church and State in Canadian Education.* Toronto: Ryerson, 1959.

Trofimenkoff, Susan Mann. *The Dream of Nation: A Social and Intellectual History of Quebec.* Toronto: Gage, 1983.

Tulchinsky, Gerald J. J. *Taking Root: The Origins of the Canadian Jewish Community.* Toronto: Lester, 1992.

Wade, Mason. *The French Canadians 1760–1967.* Toronto: Macmillan, 1968.

Wallot, Jean-Pierre. "Religion and French-Canadian Mores in the Early Nineteenth Century." *Canadian Historical Review* 52 (March 1971): 51–94.

Weaver, R. Kent, ed. *The Collapse of Canada?* Washington, D.C.: Brookings, 1992.

Westfall, William. "The Dominion of the Lord: An Introduction to the Cultural History of Protestant Ontario in the Victorian Period." *Queen's Quarterly* 83 (1976): 47–70.

Westhues, Kenneth. "Public vs. Sectarian Legitimation: The Separate Schools of the Catholic Church." *Canadian Review of Sociology and Anthropology* 13 (1976).

———. "Catholic Separate Schools: An Ambiguous Legacy." *Grail: An Ecumenical Journal* 1 (1984).

Williams, John R., ed. *Canadian Churches and Social Justice.* Toronto: Anglican Book Centre and James Lorimer, 1984.